WORKING TOGETHER IN UNITY

Managing Conflict Leading Volunteers

By

Dr. Karen Adams

Brad & Lori,
May the unity of Father, Son & Holy Spirit
always abide with you.
Ps 133:1
Karen Adams

WORKING TOGETHER IN UNITY

By Dr. Karen Adams

ISBN: 978-1-61529-032-1

Published by Vision Publishing
1672 Main St. E 109
Ramona, CA 92065

www.booksbyvision.com

DEDICATION

I dedicate this book to the men, women, and children that strive to make a difference in their communities through their volunteer efforts.

To every volunteer and volunteer leader throughout all generations today and in the ages to come,

May you be blessed beyond measure for your commitment to working together in unity to positively impact and change the kingdoms of this world.

ENDORSEMENTS

Some books are very key for a single season. Karen Adams has developed a book that can transcend seasons. *Working Together in Unity* is a resource that will help any organized structure, employee or individual understand the power of relationship. This textbook not only gives you mediation tools, but opens the door for you to understand the potential of cooperative relationship. I would suggest this book to anyone who wants to prosper in a new way.

Chuck D. Pierce
President, Global Spheres, Inc.
President, Glory of Zion International Ministries, Inc.

Dr. Adams, this is extraordinary!!! Thank you for this tremendously helpful book. I highly recommend it for every educator that leads a multi-generational team of teachers and volunteers.

Sharon D. Jones, M.Ed.
Director of Education
A+ Markem, Inc.

Working with volunteers requires a unique approach to managing your business. You must provide an environment that clearly demonstrates to volunteers that their contribution of time and energy is worthwhile and valued. For most volunteers, that knowledge is their reward. Karen's book clearly describes the importance of cultivating the relationship between the volunteer and the organization, and it provides excellent resources.

Diane McClendon
Executive Director
Dallas Human Resource Management Association; and,
The HR Southwest Conference

In WORKING TOGETHER IN UNITY: *Managing Conflict Leading Volunteers*, Karen Adams brings together a number of communication models, each of which is intended to facilitate people working together for a common goal. Her research is thorough and relevant to her topic. She has captured the essence not only of communication, but also of problem solving in nonprofit associations. I would highly recommend this book to all association leaders and even to those in the for-profit community as well.

Larry Burk, SPHR, CCP (Retired)
Formerly Field Services Manager/Regional Director,
Southwest Central, Society for Human Resource Management

FOREWORD

In Judges 5:1, 2 there is a very interesting passage of Scripture that is germane to Dr. Karen Adam's book. It reads:

"Then Deborah and Barak the son of Abinoam sang on that day, saying, 'That the leaders led in Israel, That the people volunteered, bless the Lord!'" (NAS)

The emphasis of this passage was on the amazement the people all shared, that leaders that were called, dedicated and willing leaders, actually took the lead in this situation (battle with the Canaanites) and equally amazing was that the people of God, known for their stubborn resistance and partisan tribal loyalty, actually volunteered. Bless the Lord indeed, for this was seen as the mightiest of miracles, more so than the military victory itself.

Taking the lead in any organization is difficult, but especially so when there is conflict amongst the people, either interpersonal or corporate. Resolving conflict is both an art and a science, and working to resolve conflict with volunteers is even more difficult. This is primarily due to the fact that volunteers are just that, volunteers. They have willingly signed on in a serving capacity, whether on the Board of Directors or as a mailroom clerk, and as easily as they have signed on they can just as easily sign off. Working with volunteers takes a different and perhaps a more sophisticated and tender approach than with a hire in general. Thus, conflict resolution, or even better, the prevention of conflict, requires a unique set of skills.

In this wonderfully written book, Karen Adams addresses the main issues relating to conflict management and resolution. Firstly, that it is essential to use effective communication techniques to engage the interests, goals and dreams of the volunteers, and motivate them in their voluntary service. Secondly, a strong leader works diligently at helping all volunteers work together in unity.

One would think this would be easy in a religious organization; sadly, this is often not the case and it requires a strong blending of culture, worldview and personality, especially when working with multigenerational volunteers. Finally, Karen focuses the reader's attention on developing strong, cooperative relationships, and discusses some of the logistical aspects of recruiting and managing volunteer workers and leaders.

I highly recommend this work, developed in the crucible of volunteer leadership and management. It will no doubt help solve many problems, and help a leader resolve or avoid conflict more effectively.

Dr. Stan E. DeKoven
President and Founder
Vision International University: College and Graduate School
Vision International Education Network

PREFACE and ACKNOWLEDGMENTS

WORKING TOGETHER IN UNITY: *Managing Conflict Leading Volunteers* is a textbook on conflict resolution and volunteer program administration that will prepare organizational leaders, volunteer managers and volunteer program coordinators to handle all aspects of leading a team of volunteers.

This book will impart to you the ability to integrate your newly learned interpersonal communication and conflict resolution skills to ignite and engage the four generations of volunteers in today's workplace. You will discover current trends in the usage of social media networks to communicate. You will gain insight on how to collaborate to solve problems. And, you will learn new approaches to the overall concept of volunteer program administration that include how to methodically recruit, train, and retain volunteers and volunteer leaders.

Armed with these new tools and strategies, I am confident that this book will become an important source of reference that will help you, the organizational leader, volunteer manager, or volunteer program administrator to understand, unite and ignite four generations of 21st Century volunteers!

This book reflects the knowledge and expertise that I have gained from more than 20 years of conflict resolution experience in the private sector and my ongoing service as a volunteer. It is also a product of extensive research and the collaborative efforts of many of my friends, colleagues and family members that provided constructive insight and recommendations that I hope that you, the reader, will find valuable.

I want to express my heartfelt gratitude to Dr. Stan DeKoven, Dr. Tal Klaus and the faculty at Vision International University for their support and critical evaluation of this work to ensure it met the standards of excellence that are expected in a work as important as this one. Dr. Stan, words cannot express the sincere appreciation, joyfulness and thankfulness that overcame me when you agreed to write the Foreword for this book. You are truly a blessing!

I want to thank Kathy Smith, editor extraordinaire for Vision Publishing for your guidance, advice and exemplary edits. Your finishing touches made this a much better book.

My sincere gratitude is extended to Dr. Joshua Reichard and Marty Dobkins for their artistic mastery that captured my vision for the design for the book cover. Great job!

I will be forever grateful to my apostle, Chuck Pierce and his wonderful wife Pam for their leadership, friendship, love and support. Chuck, words cannot express the gratitude and joy that overwhelmed me when I received your endorsement for this book. Thank you so very much.

Special thanks go to Sharon D. Jones, M.Ed., Larry Burk, SPHR, CCP, Diane McClendon, and Margie Knight for reading my manuscript and providing edits, comments, practical advice, and wise counsel. I truly appreciate you for your support and valuable insight.

I want to thank and honor my mother, Shirley Lynch, sisters, Sharon Jones and Crystal Blanks, brother, Markus Lynch and all of my nieces and nephews for their love and encouragement. You are always there. I cherish each and every one of you.

To my wonderful husband, Leeman Adams, I am very thankful for you and for the endless love that we share. You always see and bring out the best in me. Your support inspires confidence and motivates me to press toward my higher calling. Thank you for being my champion!

To Alex Adams, our loving son, thank you for sharing your thoughts and helping me to better understand the needs, interests and goals of Generation Y. You are truly a blessing.

And most of all, to you, the readers of this book—Thank You! I am enormously grateful for each of you.

May wisdom, understanding, love, peace and a heart to work together in unity be within each of you, always.

CONTENTS

LIST OF FIGURES

LIST OF TABLES

INTRODUCTION

WORKING TOGETHER IN UNITY: *Managing Conflict Leading Volunteers* will arm you, the leader, with the important concepts of effective communication, management, leadership and conflict resolution. Application of these powerful techniques in the execution of your daily operations will help you to create a more productive and effectual work environment. Unlike other organizations, many non-profit organizations have a unique mix of both paid and unpaid staff. It is therefore imperative that the organization's leadership team maintains unity amongst these two groups of staff. The goal of coordinating their efforts for the overall success of the organization can be most easily realized through the utilization of the concepts presented in the following pages.

Most volunteer program administrators are recruited as the result of an internal job posting, or based upon their previous volunteer experience. The term, "volunteer program administrator" is used herein to refer to all volunteer leaders, coordinators, managers, or any other title that refers to the role of a leader of volunteers.

Many volunteer administrators may not have received advanced training on leadership, conflict management or communications skills. As a result, they may not be aware of the various business management models and theories that exist to help people communicate in more powerful and persuasive ways. The utilization of these improved communication skills can help to create a harmonious environment that will make it possible to coordinate the energy and the efforts of the staff as a whole. With this in mind, we shall begin in Section 1 to lay the foundation for these important principles, and then we will build upon them in the subsequent chapters.

The goals of Section 1 are to offer instruction on how to:

- Reach today's volunteer through the use of effective communication;
- Motivate and influence others;
- Assess the effects of a person's communication behaviors on others;
- Recognize, evaluate and eliminate self-defeating habits and actions; and,
- Create a positive environment conducive to building long-lasting relationships.

To accomplish these stated goals, a series of five specially selected communication models and theories will be analyzed and discussed. Section 1 concludes with a comprehensive discussion on the Attribution Theory, judgmental biases, prejudices and passions and the Groupthink Theory.

- The goals of Section 2 are to offer instruction on how to:
- Find common ground to deal with differences, build trust, and maintain positive, harmonious relationships;
- Take an active and positive role to ensure that confrontations are resolved in a manner that does not permanently impair the relationship;
- Build higher levels of engagement, collaboration and commitment among the team members;
- Collaboratively work together to diffuse conflicts and reach win-win solutions;
- Recognize the differences in worldviews and traditions that influence communication practices and thought processing;
- Break barriers caused by micro-iniquities;
- Identify one's own biases regarding how another person's appearance, gender or ethnicity can impede communications;
- Advocate harmonious, supportive relationships across genders, cultures, religions and ethnicities;
- Understand personality styles; and,

- Build bridges across 4 generations of paid and unpaid staff members and volunteers to maintain a harmonious work environment.

- The goals of Section 3 are to offer instruction on how to:
- Effectively manage a volunteer program;
- Use critical thinking skills to resolve problems;
- Recruit, train and retain volunteers;
- Empower volunteers to behave like owners; and
- Utilize project management tools to align the volunteer program with the organization's vision.

Section 3 concludes with a discussion on purposeful leadership and provides a copy of the Universal Declaration on Volunteerism.

Managing conflict and keeping four generations of volunteers actively engaged in the 21st Century workplace is a daunting task. However, by adopting the strategies offered in this book, you will be equipped to tap into the passion and excellence that your volunteers bring to your organization. You will be known as a leader who has the knowledge, skills and ability to inspire and motivate each generation of workers and volunteers to reach their peak performance. Armed with these new tools, you will be able to creatively lead your organization's volunteer programs to their highest level of achievement!

SECTION 1 – COOPERATION BEGINS WITH

COMMUNICATION

COMMUNICATION TECHNIQUES

One of the most important resources available to any organization is its relationship among its people and constituents. Successful leaders have the ability to establish relationships and develop a network of people to accomplish the organization's vision, mission, objectives and goals. Effective communication creates an environment of cooperation, commitment, respect and trust. These building blocks are essential for organizations that are dependent upon the services of volunteers and the collaboration of community groups, special interest coalitions, informal leaders, and others to achieve their success.

As stated in the Introduction, since most volunteer program administrators are recruited as a result of an internal job posting or volunteer experience, they may not have received advanced training on leadership, conflict management or communication skills. In this chapter, various communication models and theories that can help you reach today's volunteer will be reviewed. Methods of communication specifically suited for each of the four generations in the workplace are also included. The goals of Section 1 are to offer instruction on how to:

- Reach today's volunteer through the use of effective communication.
- Motivate and influence others.
- Recognize, evaluate and eliminate self-defeating habits and actions.
- Assess the effects of a person's communication behaviors on others.

- Create a positive environment conducive to building long-lasting relationships.

VISION SETS THE TONE

A key leadership responsibility is to ensure that team members and constituents are in alignment with the organizations' direction. You can accomplish this by sharing the organization's vision and mission statements. It is important to communicate with your team and obtain their input on how they can help to reach the organization's overarching goals. Once the team buys into the organization's vision, it will be easier to gain their commitment to provide the time, energy, resources and expertise needed to see the vision realized. This is probably a good time to define the role of a mission and vision statement.

An organization's mission is its purpose, or the reason for its existence. A mission statement is a brief written summary that tells what the company provides to society. The purpose of a mission statement is to define the fundamental "unique purposes" of the company that sets it apart from other firms of its type. It identifies the services offered and the intended market for those services. A mission statement reveals who the company is and what it does. It promotes a sense of shared expectations and lays the foundation for the organization's vision statement.

A well-written vision statement will articulate the organization's values, it will communicate the organization's priorities, and it will inspire behavior and character that reflects the vision. A visual image of an organization's direction and mission, such as banners, logos and slogans can serve as a beacon to guide the volunteers, paid staff members and constituents to achieve the organization's present and future purpose and disseminate it to others. A vision statement helps everyone to form a similar mental picture of a future state.

An inspirational vision statement is particularly important for nonprofit and religious organizations because most of them rely heavily on volunteers, donations, gifts, and grants to achieve their goals. A vibrant vision statement that encompasses some of the exciting aspects of joining your organization or supporting its mission is an excellent low-cost way to promote your organization.

The vision statement sets the tone and overarching sense of purpose for your organization. It is also an excellent framework for establishing goals and objectives. It is best to discuss the mission, vision, goals and objectives with volunteers during the recruiting process to ensure they are the right fit for the position. This can reduce high turnover rates that could result from a person not understanding the roles, responsibilities and expectations of the position.

Objectives are the end result of a planned activity. They state what is to be accomplished by when and they should be quantified if possible. Objectives are established to fulfill the organization's mission. Specific activities that are necessary to accomplish the goals and objectives should be communicated and understood on the first day of the assignment to begin to create a cooperative work environment.

METHODS OF COMMUNICATION

There are various methods of communication that are available to provide meaningful and timely support, supervision, and feedback to your team. Verbal/audio/visual communication channels, such as Skype, webcasts, telephone calls, staff meetings, and face-to face contacts; and, written communication channels, such as text messages, email, social media networks, reports, blogs, and newsletters are all necessary to meet the multiple sensory needs of the communicators and respondents.

Most people have a preferred method of sending and receiving communication. Since the process to recruit and retain volunteers is directly affected through communication, it is important to choose the appropriate methods of communication that resound with the respondents.

For example, in the 20th century we went from Pre-Baby Boomers (born before 1943) to Baby Boomers (born roughly between 1943 and 1964) to Generation X (born roughly between 1965 and 1981) to Generation Y (born roughly between 1982 and 2001). These four generations of volunteers represent the current 21st century volunteer workforce. Each group is unique with respect to their preferred method of communication. Although this book focuses on these four generations, it should be noted that very soon the Millennia's or Generation Next (born after 2001) volunteers will become more actively involved and they will have a voice of their own shaped by their generational imprints.

Given the unique experience and expertise that each generation of volunteers possesses, it is important for volunteer recruiters, volunteer managers and volunteer leaders to understand how to reach the new generations of volunteers while concurrently attracting the growing number of retiring Baby Boomers and retaining the Pre-Baby Boomers.

The preferred method of communication for a Pre-Baby Boomer and a Baby Boomer is quite different from that of a Generation X (Gen X) or a Generation Y (Gen Y) and the newly emerging Generation Next or Gen @ volunteer. Each generation has a different attitude, different work style and different expectations of the physical work environment than do the other generations.

As a result of the universal roll-out of the internet in the mid to late 1980s, Gen X and Gen Y volunteers are generally very tech savvy and prefer the use of technology to communicate (text messages, emails, blogs and social media network sites). This is in sharp contrast to the Pre-Baby Boomers or Baby Boomers, who generally prefer to communicate in-person or via the telephone and receive "hard-copy" communications, such as, letters, newsletters, or notes. However, as time goes on, an increasing number of Pre-Baby Boomers and Baby Boomers have adapted to communication via email and social media networks, such as Facebook.

Determining the most effective method to communicate with a person on an individual basis will help you to cultivate a shared commitment and personal engagement among the volunteers, paid staff and constituents. In spite of present day advancements in communication methods, whether it is to use newsletters or blogs or social media networks, research has shown that a fundamental principle to master the transformation in 21st Century communications is to "concentrate on the relationships, not the technologies." (Li and Bernoff 2008, 18).

SOCIAL MEDIA NETWORKING

In their book, *"Groundswell: Winning in a World Transformed by Social Technologies"* (Li and Bernoff 2008) the authors provide extensive data and advice on how to communicate in the 21st Century. They point out how important it is for businesses to understand the magnitude and effect of the usage of the internet to connect and communicate. They state that "Even inside companies, your employees are connecting on social networks, building ideas with online collaboration tools, and discussing the pros and cons of your policies and priorities. The groundswell has changed the balance of power." (Li and Bernoff 2008, 13)

Social media networking sites are a useful method to facilitate communication through the use of technology while concurrently focusing on building and strengthening relationships. Many companies, organizations and institutions have joined Facebook, Twitter, or other social media networks to connect with their customers, members or constituents and to boost brand awareness.

Social media networks are an excellent forum for volunteers to promote charitable activities, such as walks for cancer, and other causes or organizations that they support. Social media networking sites are a good example of a strategically targeted method of communication to connect with Gen X and Gen Y volunteers because they attract visitors that have a shared interest in the organization's purpose and goals.

In *The New Breed* (McKee 2008, 17, 18), the authors stated, "In the last 20 years, we've observed six seismic shifts that have shaken the world of volunteer management and have catalyzed this new breed of volunteer." They are:

1. Family dynamics: From Father Knows Best to Gilmore Girls
2. Isolation: From community to individualism
3. Flexibility: From rigid scheduling to volunteer availability
4. Generations: From experienced veterans to novice Gen @
5. Technology: From face-to-face to cyberspace
6. Professionalism: From skilled workers to knowledge workers

The aforementioned evolution in the world of volunteer management has dictated changes in the communication methods that are used to recruit, manage, and lead the 21st Century volunteer. The variety of communication techniques, styles, and skills that are needed to reach and motivate this new breed of volunteers while continuing to engage Pre-Baby Boomers and Baby Boomers has made it even more important to understand the impact of interpersonal communications.

EFFECTIVE INTERPERSONAL COMMUNICATION

Interpersonal communication is a process of creating a mental image of a shared purpose, goal, or vision that resonates with the targeted audience and inspires a positive response. The emotional impact of the projected mental image must be the same for both the sender and the receiver in order for it to have the same impact on each person communicating.

Different emotional impacts can be derived from the same form of communication. This results in two distinctively different visual images created by the same communication which can lead to miscommunication. Because of this, it is important to involve a cross-section of stakeholders from all age groups, ethnicities and cultures, including volunteers and paid staff, to develop or review communication items before they are released. The communications that result from this shared review will help to ensure the clarity of the message.

Effective communication is the process of minimizing misunderstandings. William Gundykunst, the developer of the Anxiety/Uncertainty Management (AUM) theory wrote the following, "Communication is effective to the extent that the person interpreting the message attaches a meaning to the message that is relatively similar to what was intended by the person transmitting it." (Gudykunst 2005)

The two most dangerous and common assumptions made when conveying a message are:

- I understand
- I am being understood

Most people believe they understand what has been communicated and that they are clearly communicating what they have to say. However, research has shown that communication is a process and there are many internal and external factors that may hinder clear communications. To demonstrate how these factors impact communication it may be helpful to review various communication models that discuss the process of communication.

COMMUNICATION MODELS AND THEORIES

Communication models and theories are useful because they offer insight into behavior patterns and communication principles which will relate to most of the communication situations a person may encounter.

The communication models that were selected for this book were specifically chosen to identify the communications issues that may arise in an organizational setting where trust, integrity and honest communications are expected; but, at times, not met. The purpose of the presentation of these models is 1) to provide you with knowledge and insight into how to recognize behaviors that can lead to discord and disharmony; and, 2) to provide you with strategies on how to intervene and change those behaviors before they impact morale. These models will give you the tools that you need to proactively address behavior issues to maintain harmony in your workplace.

Five communication models and theories are reviewed in Section 1. The first communication model discussed is the sender / receiver transmission model of communications that has been referred to as the Field of Experience model. This communication model considers the impact that a person's beliefs, values, experiences and prior learning has on how a message is sent and received. The Field of Experience is a foundational communication model that explains the process of communication. A basic understanding of the process of communication will enable you to discern when you are not connecting with your intended audience.

The second theory discussed is Maslow's Hierarchy of Needs. This theory describes why it is important to meet a person's individual needs. And, it gets to the heart of why people volunteer their services. Maslow's Hierarchy of Needs pyramid provides a graphic picture of the progressive nature of motivation that allows a person to experience a sense of self-fulfillment. This section provides the key to understanding the difference between what drives people versus what people are drawn to.

The third theory discussed is the Fundamental Interpersonal Relations Orientation (FIRO) theory. This model offers insight into how a person communicates needs and interests, both directly and indirectly. The FIRO theory claims that all humans, to some degree, possess three needs: 1) the need for inclusion, 2) the need for control, and, 3) the need for affection. The value of the FIRO theory for organizations staffed by volunteers is that people volunteer to fulfill a certain need. By being aware of various aspects of personal needs and interests and how a person expresses them, you will be better equipped to provide meaningful feedback and develop rewards and recognition programs that meet the needs and interests of your volunteers.

The fourth theory is the Transactional Model. This model emphasizes the point that communication is a two-way transaction that requires both give and take. Authentic, honest communication creates a positive work environment. Staying positive in the face of

23

challenging circumstances can be difficult. However, by developing effective communication skills and by putting them into practice, an environment of cooperation, mutuality, and trust can be created and maintained.

The fifth theory discussed is the Interpersonal Deception Theory. This is an important theory to understand because in life everyone encounters both subtle and overt forms of deception. The theorists offered 18 Propositions that were well worth repeating in this section to offer guidance on how deceivers and respondents behave. A review of these 18 Propositions will illuminate situations in which you were a party to a deceptive interaction and it will provide you with guidance on how to handle these situations in the future.

FIELD OF EXPERIENCE MODEL

Communication is the process of human beings responding to the symbolic behavior of others. People do not communicate to other people, they communicate with other people.

Communication is the exchange of thoughts, messages, or information between people, by means of speech, signals, writing, or using a common system of signs or behavior. Communication is an ongoing, cyclical process. Communication is a process because it involves a sender, a receiver, message encoding, message decoding, psychological noise, physiological noise, communication channels, and communication environment.

Academic researchers have traditionally viewed communication in accordance with the sender / receiver model developed by Claude Shannon and Warren Weaver and published in 1949 in their book titled, *The Mathematical Theory of Communication.* (Shannon and Weaver 2009). Dr. Wilbur Schramm is known as a forefather in the academic field in the development of basic models of communication. His basic models are a derivation of the Shannon-Weaver transmission model of communication. The Shannon-Weaver model proposed the following elements of communication:

- sender
- message
- transmission
- noise
- channel
- reception
- receiver

Dr. Schramm's 1954 model (Schramm, The Process and Effects of Communication 1954, 3-26) expanded on the Shannon-Weaver model by emphasizing the process of interpretation (encoding and decoding the message). In addition to the elements above, Dr. Schramm depicted feedback as interactive and circular. He also incorporated the study of human behavior in the communication process. As such, he published the following diagrams to reflect his research:

Diagram of Dr. Schramm's Interactive Model, 1954

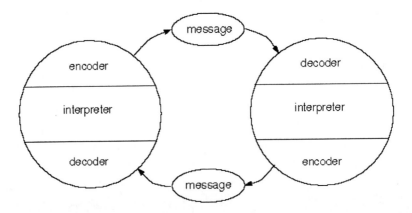

In the above model, the sender encodes the message by translating his ideas, feelings, and intentions into a message appropriate for sending. The message is transmitted to the receiver. The receiver decodes the message by interpreting its meaning. The receiver's interpretation depends on how well the receiver understands the content of the message and the intentions of the sender. The receiver responds internally to this interpretation of the message and then becomes the sender, which means he encodes the message by translating his ideas, feelings, and intentions into a response appropriate for sending and responds with feedback.

Feedback is initiated by a receiver in response to a message received which influences the subsequent behavior of the original sender. Feedback may be: positive or negative; immediate or delayed; verbal or nonverbal; or intentional or unintentional. Two-way communication occurs when the sender is able to obtain feedback concerning how the receiver is decoding the sender's message.

Dr. Schramm's Field of Experience "How Communication Works" model (Schramm, The Process and Effects of Mass Communication 1961, 5-6) further captures the sender / receiver model and it reflects the interconnectedness between the sender and receiver's communication.

Diagram of Dr. Schramm's Field of Experience model.

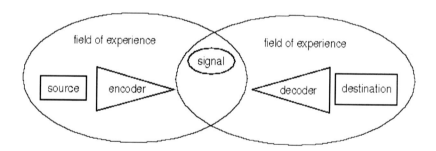

Dr. Schramm's research suggests that a message can be complicated by different meanings learned by different people. Effective communication exists between two people when the receiver interprets the sender's message the way the sender intended it. Your field of experience, meaning your individual beliefs, values, experiences and prior learning impacts how you send and receive a message.

VERBAL AND NON-VERBAL IMPEDIMENTS TO COMMUNICATION

The interpretation of any communication is influenced by the meanings attributed to the words that are used. Meanings can be *denotative* or *connotative*. Denotative meanings are the most specific or direct meaning of a word, such as a dictionary definition, and they generally have the same meaning for most people. Connotative meanings are implied or evaluative and they are based on personal experience or a meaning suggested by or associated with a word or a thing.

In addition to unintended errors in word interpretation, the communication process is further impacted by verbal and non-verbal messages sent by the sender or received by the receiver. The sender's attitude, prejudices, frame of mind or appropriateness of language can hamper effective communication. Or, for the receiver, the communication could be impeded by the sender's speech problems, such as stammering or mumbling, or annoying or distracting gestures. Accurate listening can be further confused by any of the other links in the sender / receiver communication process.

Some other characteristics of messages that impact effective communication between two people are factors, such as, environmental sounds (TV, radio, traffic, or static), intelligence levels, cultural backgrounds, emotional readiness, verbal cues, vocal cues, and visual cues.

Verbal cues include words that are unambiguous, descriptive, explicit, redundant, simple, thorough, organized, or direct. Vocal cues include the rapidity or slowness of speech, the volume and pitch of the person's voice, the inflections, enunciation and pleasantness or unpleasantness of the person's voice.

Visual cues include facial expressions, such as winking, frowning and smiling, body language, such as posture, eye contact, body movement, such as leaning forward, moving away, touching, and even clothing, jewelry (e.g. crosses, skulls), body piercing, tattoos and hairstyles can impact communication. The successful transmission of a message depends on whether the message will be accepted over all the competing messages.

ACTIVE LISTENING

Even when a message is successfully transmitted it is not always heard because the receiver is formulating a response concurrent with the message being transmitted. Often this occurs during an argument or when a person is very passionate about a subject and is trying to persuade the other person to agree. When this happens, each person tends to be more focused on stating his or her position rather than listening to what the other person has to say which is counterproductive to effective communications. A better approach would be to listen and acknowledge the other person's view and then, without challenging it, calmly express the differing view.

At times, a person is merely seeking an empathetic listener and does not want to engage in a dialogue. The role of an empathetic listener is to listen with an accepting ear and relinquish the desire to fix people. An empathetic listener should listen with unconditional acceptance and not analyze or admonish the other person. As an empathetic listener you should avoid asking "Why?" questions because these questions are loaded with implied criticism. Words are often perceived as judgmental and attacking. Therefore the use of non-judgmental, emotionally neutral words is the best way to respond empathetically.

Although sender / receiver models for communication allow for a process of interpreting the message, it is important to note that they also recognize that interpretations are influenced by some level of overlapping experience to achieve successful communication. Therefore, communications should be tailored to address the complementary experiences of the sender and receiver. An example of how you could accomplish this would be to include value statements in communications that tap into your team member's sense of purpose and their needs and desires to be a part of your organization.

SUMMARY

We began this chapter by stating that one of the most important resources available to any organization is its relationships. The relationships of the people and the constituents help to maintain a sense of unity and cohesiveness among the organization's people, while serving to strengthen and support the group as a whole. Organizations that are staffed by both paid and unpaid staff (such as a Board of Directors or elected officers at a non-profit organization) have an even greater need for effective interpersonal communication. This is true for the following reasons:

1. To ensure the volunteers feel appreciated for their contributions;
2. To ensure the organization's values are reflected in every aspect of its communications; and,
3. To create an environment of cooperation, mutuality, respect and trust.

In this chapter various aspects of communication were discussed including verbal cues, vocal cues, and visual cues. Examples of verbal cues, such as choice of words; vocal cues, such as tone of voice; and visual cues, such as frowning, smiling and making eye contact were provided. The influence that clothing, jewelry (e.g. crosses or skulls), body piercing, tattoos and hairstyles can have on communication and the perceived image of an organization was also cited. This chapter also provided valuable insight into how to establish long-lasting relationships and develop a network of people through the use of various communication models.

The next chapter builds on these communication principles. It provides insight on how to understand and recognize a person's personal needs and interests. Organizations that build upon these foundational interpersonal relationship models will find that their unique communication needs are being successfully met to the benefit of all.

PERSONAL NEEDS, INTERESTS, AND GOALS

Volunteers have an earnest desire to serve and to make a meaningful difference in the organizations they choose to support. Volunteers invest their time and sometimes even their money into these organizations. They do so to meet their own personal need to contribute to the success of the organization, institution, or cause that they champion. The successful implementation of a volunteer program requires providing of opportunities for the volunteers to share their insights and to bond together with the entire team of workers. An organization that informs its volunteers of how their work benefits its mission is more apt to satisfy the personal needs of its volunteers. As a result, their volunteers will be more motivated to achieve the overall mission of the organization.

HIERARCHY OF NEEDS

Psychologist Abraham Maslow believed that people are basically trustworthy, responsible, self-protecting, and self-governing. His views about people are similar to those held in most nonprofit and religious organizations and by the volunteers that support them. Volunteers want to be empowered. They do not want to be managed, they want to be led. Once their basic needs for survival are met, they want to move to their highest level of achievement, which Maslow calls, self-actualization.

Maslow's Hierarchy of Needs theory states that there are four types of needs that must be satisfied before a person can act unselfishly. As shown below, the needs are arranged in a hierarchical order:

ABRAHAM MASLOW
HIERARCHY OF NEEDS

Maslow, A. Motivation and
Personality (2nd ed.)
Harper & Row, 1970.

SELF-
ACTUALIZATION
Pursue Inner Talent
Creativity Fulfillment

SELF-ESTEEM
Achievement Mastery
Recognition Respect

BELONGING - LOVE
Friends Family Spouse Lover

SAFETY
Security Stability Freedom from Fear

PHYSIOLOGICAL
Food Water Shelter Warmth

The upward climb in Maslow's Hierarchy of Needs is made by satisfying one set of needs at a time. The most basic set of needs are deficiency needs: the needs for food, water, shelter, warmth, safety, security, stability, freedom from fear, love and self-esteem. The ultimate need is the need for self-actualization.

People are driven to satisfy the lower needs as shown on the graph above. But as they meet the most basic needs they are then drawn to meet the higher level ones. This is an important distinction to understand when dealing with volunteers. They are drawn to volunteer on the basis of personal need. While their selection of a particular organization may be made according to how it meets their basic self-serving needs, (such as the need to belong and to establish relationships), they will choose to stay because they are passionate about the organization's cause. They will serve the organization of their choice in pursuit of their own need for self-fulfillment.

Maslow referred to the four lower needs as deficiency needs because the lack of needs being met causes tension within people.

In *A First Look at Communication Theory,* the author, Em Griffin wrote,

> The urge to fulfill needs is potent but not overpowering. Maslow thought that the Freudian label *instinct* overstated the case. Maslow used the term *instinctoid* to designate a less insistent motivational force. People can resist the pull of physiological, safety, love and esteem needs, but it's not easy. The instinctoid label also means that these needs are universal urges and not created by culture, as the behaviorist would claim. Although everyone has the same set of needs, our ways of fulfilling those needs can be different. (E. Griffin, A First Look at Communication Theory, Second Edition 1994, 126)

While the lower level needs are important within an organizational setting because they deal with salary, benefits, safety, security and inclusion, the esteem and self-actualization rungs on the ladder are the two needs that inspire volunteers the most. Since volunteers are generally unpaid and do not receive tangible benefits such as healthcare, pension, and so on, security needs are not as important.

Esteem needs encompass both self-esteem and the need for power. Self-esteem refers to the need for personal achievement which is the result of competency or the mastery of tasks. Power needs relates to the attention and recognition that comes from the desire to receive admiration from others. While it is important for an organization to be staffed with people that possess the knowledge, skills and abilities to competently perform the tasks that are essential to successfully executing the day-to-day activities and implementing both the short-term and long-term goals of the institution. It is equally important to value the staff members and provide the attention and recognition that is needed to motivate and inspire them to exceed the minimum expectations of their daily interactions.

Self-Actualization

One way to inspire others is to tap into their personal need for self-actualization. Maslow described self-actualization as "the desire to become more and more what one is, to become everything that one is capable of becoming." (E. Griffin, A First Look at Communication Theory, Second Edition 1994, 130)

People inherently want to maximize their potential. To tap into this desire, Maslow would ask people to describe the single most joyous, happy or blissful moment of their life. Maslow's view that self-actualization is the ultimate goal offers at least one explanation for why some people take great risks to pursue self-fulfillment.

To fill the voids in their lives, some people may choose to participate in activities such as extreme sports that involve a higher level of danger, while others may pursue philanthropic endeavors in a quest to improve the world or mankind. Other people may choose to become missionaries and worldwide evangelists to satisfy their need for fulfillment. Whatever the choice, the quest to find meaning, understanding, knowledge, beauty, peace and purpose in one's life can be a strong impetus. It can provide a sense of worth that comes from doing something of lasting value.

Maslow's theory emphasizes the freedom of choice and human goodness. Each person can choose to make responsible, unselfish commitments to others. His theory promotes the idea that once legitimate human needs have been met, then humanity has the capacity to be trustworthy, loyal, helpful, friendly, loving, and kind. The common desire for love and acceptance is a potent motivational force that drives people to live and work together in harmony.

FUNDAMENTAL INTERPERSONAL RELATIONS ORIENTATION (FIRO)

Most volunteers are motivated by their beliefs. They become involved in an organization or ministry because they believe in what it represents. While some volunteers will remain committed to an organization or ministry, no matter what, (because they believe they were divinely called to serve), others will become disengaged because their individual needs and their personal interests have not been met. Thus, it is important for volunteer program administrators to understand how to effectively fulfill the individual needs of their staff.

The Fundamental Interpersonal Relations Orientation (FIRO) theory that was developed by William Schultz (Schultz 1991) claims that all humans possess three basic needs: 1) the need for inclusion; 2) the need for control; and, 3) the need for affection.

According to Schultz, the need for inclusion is the inner drive "to establish and maintain a satisfactory relationship with people with respect to interaction and association." (Schultz 1991, 93).

Need For Inclusion

A person that has a high-level of need for inclusion places a premium on face-to-face interactions and needs to feel significant within a group setting. It is important for them to feel a sense of acceptance, of belonging, and of group togetherness. This person places a high value on receiving respect and validation of self-worth. Given their need for personal interaction, the use of email as a primary form or communication would not be an effective communication tool. It is better to provide an "open door" environment where ideas can be freely shared and are welcomed. Volunteers do not want to simply contribute to the cause; they want to be asked how they can help the organization achieve its mission.

The need for inclusion can work in two ways, either by receiving or by expressing inclusion. Not only does this person want to be included, he may also have a need to reach out to other people so they won't feel isolated or lonely. People with a high need for inclusion may also have a desire to feel worthwhile by making others feel important. According to Schultz, if a person has attained a comfortable level of inclusion in both directions, he can be expected to exhibit normal social behavior in a group setting. If not, then he will tend to exhibit introverted (shy) or extroverted (boisterous) behaviors as an expression of the unfulfilled need to feel important.

Need For Control

The second interpersonal need in the FIRO triad is the need for control. Schultz defines this as "the need to establish and maintain a satisfactory relationship with people with respect to control and power." (Schultz 1991, 94) The need for control can also be expressed in two ways. It can be expressed as a strong desire to be in control or it could be a desire to be submissive and allow others to be in control. For example, a team member that has a need to be in control may make a subtle attempt to lead and direct the flow of projects through persuasion or they may volunteer to lead committees. That person may also volunteer to serve on the board of directors or as an elder.

A person with a need for control will generally possess the ability to make things happen or to bring about the desired outcomes. In volunteer organizations, the volunteer program administrator would want to look for a person that can favorably influence others to accomplish the organization's goals. The benefits of having a person that properly uses the need for control can be evidenced by the positive effect this person can have on morale and the heightened commitment of the other volunteers.

The other side of this equation is when people choose to be led by others. They gladly relinquish their own authority to enable others to take the leadership role. They are comfortable being a follower. This person (especially if it's a man) is often stereotyped as a 'wimp', when in fact he should be seen as a trusting, respectful, submissive person that has a willingness to serve. These people have a penchant to serve and are an asset to any organization. Organizations need people that exhibit both of these spectrums, both those that lead and those that follow, in order to be successful.

Need For Affection

The final interpersonal need of the FIRO triad is the need for affection. It is defined as "the need to establish and maintain a satisfactory relationship with others with respect to love and affection." (Schultz 1991, 94) This need is expressed by a person's quest to develop friendships and the need to be seen as lovable. People that need affection will measure success by positive feelings rather than by task accomplishment. Although they have a strong need to receive affection and validation, they are not always a person that reciprocates with warmth and affection towards others. Positive reinforcement and appreciative feedback makes them feel nurtured and loved. They need both to stay engaged and motivated.

Schultz's FIRO categories of inclusion, control and affection reflect some of the different needs and interests that motivate people. His FIRO-B questionnaire (available from Consulting Psychologists Press, Inc. at www.cpp.com) is a tool that can be used to assess social needs and a person's motive profile. It can aid in predicting interpersonal behavior in group settings. However, it should be noted that people can and do change. A person has the ability to freely determine the amount of inclusion, control and affection that person chooses to extend to others. The value of the FIRO theory for organizations that rely on both paid staff and volunteers is that people tend to volunteer to fulfill a certain specific need.

By being aware of the various communication models that deal with personal needs and interests, the organizational leaders and the volunteer program administrators will be better equipped to provide meaningful feedback. This will enable them to develop rewards and recognition programs that meet the needs of its entire staff.

COMMUNICATION TRANSACTIONS

An essential requirement for building a lasting relationship is to be trustworthy. People are willing to follow those that they respect and trust. Personal leadership qualities that earn the trust of others include integrity, honesty, confidence, maturity, competence, ethics, and well established values. The term "values" as used here means the worth or the importance a person places on people, things, ideas, beliefs, or principles.

Organizational values must be integrated with the values of the staff members and the volunteers in organizations to successfully execute their daily operations, especially since a volunteer's values are a primary motivator for being a part of the organization. An organization's values should be clearly communicated in writing and be visibly displayed. The purpose of this communication is to build trust and a strong alliance between an institution and an individual.

Leadership is a two-way street. On the one hand, the institution's leadership team must focus on the organizational plans and goals, while on the other hand they must consider the impact of their decisions on the individual's needs and desires.

In a model developed by Getzels and Guba, (Getzels and Guba 2002) partially depicted below, they diagram the balance that is required within and between institutions and individuals. The flow of their model shows how social systems (institutions and individuals) behave horizontally and vertically.

The institution → Role → Role Expectations

$\uparrow\downarrow$ $\uparrow\downarrow$ $\uparrow\downarrow$

The individual → Personality → Need-Dispositions

In this model, the institution represents the overarching entity (which is run by the leadership team), and the individual represents each person that is an employee (paid or unpaid) of that organization. This model reflects the interrelatedness between the behavior of the institution and that of the individual and how it has a direct impact on their interactions in meeting each other's expectations.

Open communications, both horizontally and vertically, are important to fully comprehend the role expectations and need dispositions. When roles and needs are clearly understood and agreed upon, then the individuals are more likely to take ownership of their assigned tasks and work together to see that they are accomplished. Today's volunteer leaders have to be flexible and willing to listen to each individual, and they must be willing to empower them to do the job. Their goal should be to lead in such a way that the volunteers are telling others about the positive experiences they are having from working at the organization.

EMPOWERMENT

The success of the institution lies with the effectiveness of its leadership team. Leadership ability, for better or worse, always has an impact on organizational effectiveness. "Effective leadership moves an organization toward fulfillment of its vision and empowers those who participate in that effort...With empowerment, people feel like an important part of a team or community, they make a contribution to the organization's success, they value learning and competence, and they find that the work changes and energizes them. Empowerment adds to volunteers' sense of significance and value to the organization and emphasizes their capabilities." (Fisher and Cole 1993, 10) Empowerment is vital to organizations because it strengthens interpersonal relationships and fosters an atmosphere of cooperation.

A theoretical underpinning of Getzels and Guba's model is the idea of Role Theory. The Role Theory formulates the need to provide tangible evidence of role expectations in the form of formal job descriptions and written work environment / employment policies. These job descriptions and policy statements are designed to effectively express the prescribed role and expectations of each position or job within the organization and to set expectations for workplace conduct.

Equally important are the less formal expectations derived not from official policy delineation and expression, but, rather, from the unspoken and undocumented expectations. These more subtle and less overt expectations may be more powerful and influential than the formal job descriptions. For example, at some non-profit institutions, although attendance at after-hours company sponsored fund-raising events is "voluntary", a person that does not attend these events may not be seen by others as a committed team player. As a result, when promotion or special recognition opportunities arise, it is likely that this person will not be selected. Therefore, it is important that these unofficial role expectations, that are implicit and inherent in the specific context of the job itself, be understood to avoid confusion.

Although a primary tenet of the Role Theory is to create stability, an organization's leaders must be willing to be open to change and avoid rigidity in coping with the tension that may arise when individual needs or institutional expectations are not being met. The successful operation of an organization is a transactional proposition that requires cooperation and flexibility on the part of the institution's leaders and the individual team members. A major barrier to success is the fear of change or the lack of imagination.

Successful leaders are learners. They are willing to take risks to achieve and maintain harmony for both the individual and the institution. They know that they must listen to others and be able to work cooperatively with staff members at all levels in the organization to facilitate positive relationships between the staff and volunteers. They understand that if they are willing to empower those who do the work to accomplish the organization's goals and vision, that along the way each person will have an opportunity to achieve the fulfillment of the needs and interests that motivated them to join the organization in the first place.

SUMMARY

Navigating the new dynamic communication environment in the 21st Century requires that leaders be forward thinking and actively engaged. The selection of the most effective method to communicate based upon one's individual needs is a powerful way to strengthen relationships and cultivate shared commitment and personal engagement among volunteers, paid staff and constituents.

Three communication models and theories were discussed. They were chosen to specifically address the needs, interests and aspirations of the volunteers to help keep them motivated and energized, and to provide practical suggestions on how to maintain harmony among the paid staff and the volunteers. Each of these models stresses the importance of the institution's leaders and the individuals working together to achieve harmony within the organization.

The next chapter will expand upon interpersonal communications by delving deeper into motivation techniques that are effective in leading and motivating four generations of volunteers in the 21st Century workplace. There is also an important discussion on how ethics impacts relationships. Chapter 3 concludes with an analysis of the Interpersonal Deception Theory. This is an important theory to understand because in life everyone encounters both subtle and overt forms of deception. This theory reveals how to recognize and respond to falsification, concealment and equivocation while concurrently maintaining a positive relationship.

MOTIVATION AND LEADERSHIP

Today's volunteer has a unique temperament, character and style. They want to be actively involved and want to provide input on organizational management, strategic planning and implementation, and the opportunity to assist in the daily activities of an organization. They are committed to helping the organization accomplish its mission and they want to be empowered to make a difference.

Volunteers supplement the efforts of paid staff in schools, child care facilities, family centers, hospitals, health related facilities, churches, prisons, recreation centers, disaster relief organizations and numerous other nonprofit institutions and membership organizations. Thus, it may be helpful to begin by describing some of the characteristics of the 21st Century volunteer and the reasons why they choose to volunteer. We will follow this with a discussion on motivational techniques.

THE 21ST CENTURY VOLUNTEER

In *The New Breed*, the authors provide the following description of "The New Breed Volunteer" (McKee 2008, 24):

The new breed of volunteer:

- Is very busy, has many obligations, and often volunteers for multiple organizations.
- Wants flexibility.
- Expects to be empowered.
- Won't tolerate working alongside incompetent volunteers.
- Is tech savvy.
- Doesn't want to simply make a contribution; the new breed of volunteer wants to make a difference.
- Doesn't want to be micromanaged.

The 21st Century volunteer has a strong desire for authority and autonomy. Today's volunteer asks questions, such as, "How much autonomy do I have over my time?" "How much autonomy do I have over how I complete the task?" "Will I have input on improving the current technique?" "Can I decide which team I will work with?" Today's volunteer is very committed but they are also entrepreneurial and want to be empowered so they can take ownership for their own accomplishments.

One item on the aforementioned list, "won't tolerate working alongside incompetent volunteers" is a reflection of the strong work ethic that volunteers bring to an organization. Research shows that peers observe more examples of work behavior across a variety of situations than supervisors and that their assessment of their counterparts ranges from supportive to brutally honest. Research also shows that poor performing workers can have a negative impact on morale and it may depreciate the motivation of coworkers.

Managers are responsible to ensure that the work gets accomplished and that poor performance is not overlooked. Volunteers, like paid staff, expect leaders to deal with poor performers. An array of employee engagement tools that can be used to achieve peak performance from both the volunteers and staff members are discussed in the chapter titled "21st Century Volunteer Leadership."

REASONS WHY VOLUNTEERS VOLUNTEER

According to the authors of *Leading Today's Volunteers: Motivate and Manage Your Team,* (MacLeod and Hogarth 1999, 4-5), some of the reasons people volunteer are because they like to –

- Help Others
- Help a cause they believe in
- Do something they like to do
- Develop their ability to relate to and care for others
- Do work that benefits their children, family, or themselves
- Give something back to the community
- Feel they accomplish something
- Achieve personal growth

- Meet people and find new friends
- Use their skills in a new setting
- Learn new skills
- Find challenge in new experiences
- Gain work experience
- Network
- Demonstrate commitment to and further their career goals

The authors continue by stating,

"People want new experiences, new friends and colleagues, challenges, personal development, career contacts, and especially new skills. But people also have a range of reasons for volunteering that relate closely to personally held goals and values. They are concerned about the quality of life in their community. They want to participate in a meaningful way, give something back, improve the community by identifying new social issues and gaps in services, and they feel they can have a direct and personal impact on the world. Volunteering provides a channel for skills, aspirations, interests, and concerns that may not have an outlet in their work or home life." (MacLeod and Hogarth 1999, 5)

Armed with the above information on what motivates a volunteer, an organization's leadership team and the volunteer program administrator can design recruitment and retention strategies that will fulfill the needs, interests and desires of its volunteers.

Volunteers want to be empowered and treated like a valued professional. It is important for the volunteer program administrators to keep this in mind so that they can devise and implement appropriate forms of motivational and reward incentives. These incentives can then be effectively utilized once the volunteers are on board to recognize their accomplishments and expertise.

MOTIVATIONAL TECHNIQUES

Motivational techniques will vary based upon the individual and the individual's performance. Most methods of motivation are rooted in the law of Cause and Effect, meaning the organization punishes the behavior it wants to eliminate and it rewards the behavior it wants to continue. In general, there are three types of motivation.

1. Fear motivation – Fear motivation is coercive and to be successful, it relies on the willingness of people to submit to pressure. It is enforced by either the negative reinforcement principle or punishment. Negative reinforcement (If I do this, then that won't happen) is a form of self-motivation whereby negative outcomes are avoided by performing a specific action. Whereas, punishment is a penalty that is imposed for doing something wrong. The use of punishment always involves an element of unpleasantness for both the administrator and the recipient.

2. Incentive motivation – A tangible reward that has value to the recipient who is rewarded for desirable behavior. The types of rewards will vary based on the recipient. They can be monetary (pay raise, stock options), symbolic (trophy, plaque, medal), tangible gifts (baseball tickets, country club membership), or an award specific and unique to the individual (recognized in newsletter or at a banquet). The shortcoming of incentive motivation is that once awarded it loses its motivational force and a promised award that motivates today may not motivate the person in the future.

3. Attitude motivation – Is based on the satisfaction of individual needs. Attitude motivation is an exchange system. It is mutual giving and receiving. Each individual's needs are different. Psychological needs, such as, self esteem, acceptance, status, personal worth, belonging, and security are examples of needs that

encompass an attitude motivation. Meeting a person's psychological needs takes time and involves developing a relationship with that person.

Attitude motivation is an effective long-term form of motivation. Thus, it should be used in organizations that have both paid staff members and volunteers because of the emphasis this technique has on the development of relational bonds in building strong, harmonious teams. Suggestions that you can use to accomplish these relational bonds are:

- Personal authenticity – Be yourself around others. This is the key to being able to relate to others.
- Be approachable.
- Learn about the families of coworkers. Compliment them on the achievements of their children. Congratulate them on births, weddings. Express condolences when a family member dies.
- Inquire about the health of a family member who was ill.
- Ask for their input and suggestions about how to solve problems when they arise.
- Greet people by name when you see them and smile!
- Take note of an action indicating initiative and express your appreciation.
- Offer words of encouragement and belief in people.
- Celebrate success!

Today's volunteer is more apt to stay motivated in organizations that embrace creativity, innovation, technology, flexibility, diversity and that provide an opportunity to make a meaningful difference. Time and energy should be spent to maintain rapport with volunteers, and they should be provided with a positive work environment. The work environment within an organization is often determined by its ethics. The role that ethics play in decision making will influence the behavior of the people that interact with and within the organization.

Good decisions influence morale, trust and productivity. The decisions made by an organization's leadership team will have far reaching effects on the success of the organization, the lives of the individuals, and the organizational culture. Two key questions about decision making which should be made in any organization are:

- What role do ethics play in decision making?
- How can ethical decision making be improved?

A company that sets and maintains high ethical standards is more likely to have highly engaged motivated workers.

ETHICS

Personal and organizational ethics are influenced by factors such as: magnitude of consequences; probability of effect; social consensus; temporal immediacy; proximity; justification, and balancing multiple interests. Any of these factors can impact the decisions made by an organization's employees.

Every organization should have a written statement or code of ethics which it follows. In addition to the organization's stated ethics that express the values of the organization to its employees and outside entities, there are also well established ethical principles that can help to guide an organization's conduct.

For example, there are ethical principles that justify self-serving behaviors and decisions, such as the Human/Equal Rights principle that provides common rights for all people. There are also ethical principles that focus on how to balance multiple interests, such as, the Means-End principle. This principle espouses rationalizations for actions taken to attain an ultimate goal such as peace or happiness.

There is also the Professional Ethics principle (e.g. doctor-patient confidentiality); or ethical principles that consider the affected parties and the public, such as the Disclosure principle (e.g. Sarbanes-Oxley). Finally there is the overarching biblical ethic principle – the Golden Rule, which tells us to do unto others as we would have others do unto us.

Many of the above listed ethical principles, such as those that justify self-serving behaviors and the means-justifies-the-end principle can have far-reaching consequences. For example, there are some people in the United Nations that believe that peace should be achieved at all costs, including giving away land, changing lawful boundaries or going to war. Does relinquishing one's inheritance justify peace? Does war justify peace?

Or in the medical profession, there are those that believe a person has a right to die with the assistance of medication. Does a person have a right to decide when to die? Should birth control or abortions be provided to minors without their parent's knowledge? Any one of these ethical choices can cause conflict and dissension within organizations and among its people. Of course, not all ethical decisions arise to the level of contention that these examples may invoke. These examples are only intended to illustrate the wide-range of implications that ethics has in our society and why it is important to understand the role ethics plays when decisions are made.

Ethical decision making should be integrated into an organization's daily life. Top management should commit to and model ethical behavior and they should expect all of their employees (both paid staff and volunteers) to adhere to the organization's code of ethics. Procedures should be established for the organization's members to report unethical behavior without fear of reprisal.

Unfortunately, despite an organization's best efforts, some people will choose to behave in unethical ways and attempt to cover-up their behavior. Some people will cross ethical lines in an effort to achieve personal success, to "save face," or to maintain relationships.

At times, the desire for affiliation or acceptance can influence people to make statements that are less than completely honest in order to avoid hurting or offending another person. For example, a person may offer an insincere compliment in response to a question such as, "How do you like my new hairstyle?" Or there are those that may not provide a direct answer to a question, such as, "What time did you come in?" to hide the fact that they were late for work. Or an employee may understate the cost of goods or services to conceal going over budget. People that do these things are often motivated by a need or desire to avoid conflict or maintain harmonious relationships, albeit through deceptive communication. Oftentimes, this is referred to as a "white lie."

In my book, *Life in the Matrix: Are you really in control of your decisions?* (Adams 2010, 76-77), I wrote the following regarding the biblical spiritual weapon referred to Ephesians 6:14 (NIV) as "the belt of truth":

"We should not compromise the truth, twist the truth, or rationalize our behavior under the guise of ignorance or relativism. There is no such thing as a white lie…Be willing to admit when you are untruthful rather than hiding, denying, or shifting the blame to others. Own up to your faults without making excuses…The belt of truth is a sure-fire way to stand firm against deception. However, we can't just put it on and take it off when it suits us. We have to wear it at all times."

INTERPERSONAL DECEPTION THEORY

It is human nature to expect others to tell the truth. This is called, "truth bias." People inherently want to believe what they are told. One reason people are easily fooled is due to an implied social contract that people will be honest with each other (truth bias), especially people who know and like each other. This also explains why people will sometimes overlook or explain away statements that others might find questionable. As stated above, in an effort to maintain relationships or "save face" some people will intentionally be deceptive. This behavior has been studied and the researchers have developed a theory that is referred to as the "Interpersonal Deception Theory."

David Buller and Judee Burgoon developed the Interpersonal Deception Theory. (Buller and Burgoon 2006) According to their theory, based upon any given circumstance that a person may encounter, people often find themselves in situations where they make less than honest statements, "to avoid hurting or offending another person, to emphasize their best qualities, to avoid getting into a conflict, or to speed up or slow down a relationship." (Buller and Burgoon 2006, 97)

Buller and Burgoon believe people actively participate in verbal deceit which they label as falsification, concealment and equivocation. By their definition, falsification creates a fiction, concealment hides a secret and equivocation dodges the issue. All three are a form of interpersonal deception which they define as "a message knowingly transmitted by a sender to foster a false belief or conclusion by the receiver." (Buller and Burgoon 2006, 98)

The Interpersonal Deception Theory includes 18 Propositions which offer to "explain the interplay between active deceivers and detectors who communicate with multiple motives, who behave strategically, whose communication behaviors mutually influence one another to produce a sequence of moves and countermoves, and whose communication is influenced by the situation in which the deception transpires." (Buller and Burgoon 2006, 99)

Following is an abridged and paraphrased version of the 18 "Propositions of Interpersonal Deception Theory." The term leakage as used herein refers to unconscious nonverbal cues that signal an internal state. (Buller and Burgoon 2006, 100-101):

1. What deceivers and respondents think and do varies according to the amount of interactive give-and-take that's possible in the situation.
2. What deceivers and respondents think and do varies according to how well they know and like each other.
3. Deceivers make more strategic moves and leak more nonverbal cues than truth tellers.
4. With increased interaction, deceivers make more strategic moves and display less leakage.

5. Deceivers and respondents expectation for honesty (truth bias) is positively linked with interactivity and relational warmth.

6. A deceiver's fear of being caught and the strategic activity that goes with that fear are lower when truth bias is high, and vice versa.

7. Motivation affects strategic activity and leakage. (a) People who deceive for their own self-gain make more strategic moves and display more leakage. (b) The way the respondent first reacts depends on the relative importance of the relationship and their initial suspicion.

8. As relational familiarity increases, deceivers become more afraid of detection, make more strategic moves, and display more leakage.

9. Skilled deceivers appear more believable because they make more strategic moves and display less leakage than unskilled deceivers.

10. A deceiver's perceived credibility is positively linked to interactivity, the respondent's truth bias, and the deceiver's communication skill, but goes down to the extent that the deceiver's communication is unexpected.

11. A respondent's accuracy in spotting deception goes down when interactivity, the respondent's truth bias, and the deceiver's communication skill go up. Detection is positively linked to the respondent's listening skills, relational familiarity, and the degree to which the deceiver's communication is unexpected.

12. Respondents' suspicion is apparent in their strategic activity and leakage.

13. Deceivers spot suspicion when it's present. Perception of suspicion increases when a respondent's behavior is unexpected. Any respondent reactions that signal disbelief, doubt, or the need for more information increase the deceiver's perception of suspicion.

14. Real or imagined suspicion increases deceivers' strategic activity and leakage.

15. The way deception and suspicion are displayed within a given interaction changes over time.
16. In deceptive interactions, reciprocity is the most typical pattern of adaptive response.
17. When the conversation is over, the respondent's detection accuracy, judgment of deceiver credibility, and truth bias depend on the deceiver's final strategic moves and leakage as well as the respondent's listening skill and remaining suspicions.
18. When the conversation is over, the deceiver's judgment of success depends on the respondent's final reaction and the deceiver's perception of lasting suspicion.

At the root, deception is an attempt to control or influence someone or something in an ingenious or devious way. Whether through falsification, concealment, or equivocation, the deceptive act is a lie. A successful deceiver must consciously manipulate information to create a plausible message, present it in a sincere manner, monitor reactions to the message, and provide an appropriate follow-up response.

The theorists postulate that every deceptive act has at least three aims—to accomplish a specific task, to establish or maintain a relationship with the respondent, and to "save face" or sustain the image of one or both parties. The theorists list four message characteristics that reflect strategic intent that marks the communication as less than honest.

1 Uncertainty and vagueness – provide short, noncommittal responses.
2 Nonimmediacy, reticence, and withdrawal – symbolically remove oneself from the situation through non-verbal actions.
3 Disassociation – distance oneself from what one has done by shifting much of the responsibility to others.
4 Image and relationship protecting behavior – intentionally suppress bodily cues that might signal deception or try to appear sincere by excessive grinning, smiling (similar to

Jim Carrey's character in the film *Liar, Liar*). (Buller and Burgoon 2006, 102)

In *A First Look at Communication Theory* by Em Griffin, the author offers the following comments on the Interpersonal Deception Theory:

"Those who desire a clear-cut way to separate truth telling from deception might hope that these four telltale signs of strategic messages would provide an either / or litmus test for discerning honesty. But the world of interpersonal communication is not that simple. Almost all communication is intentional, goal directed, and mindful . . . deceptive communication is simply more so.

Multiple factors strongly affect the extent of a deceiver's strategic behavior . . . this plan-based activity increases when the situation is highly interactive, when the parties know each other well, when the deceiver particularly fears discovery, when the deceiver's motivation is selfish and when the deceiver has good communication skills." (Buller and Burgoon 2006, 103)

People are hesitant to doubt the words of close friends, close associates, or family members. When they have questions, they may tend to avoid direct confrontation in order to hide their suspicions. Instead of direct challenges, they may passively probe for more information rather than actively pursuing it. This is particularly true when the person wants to maintain the relationship.

Even when a person has doubts about what someone else has said, it may still make sense to maintain a truth bias because ultimately people who expect honesty have a better chance of getting it.

Whatever the person's motivation may be, deceptive communication is both a moral and ethical issue that can harm relationships and destroy trust. It is much better to speak the truth in love.

SUMMARY

Volunteers today have a different style of communication than they did 30 years ago. Understanding the unique temperament, character and calling of today's volunteers and how to keep them motivated and supportive of the institution's vision and goals was discussed and practical suggestions were provided for the volunteer leader.

In addition to the theoretical discussion on motivation, Chapter 3 provided practical application and suggestions on how to motivate others, specifically the 21st Century volunteer. Included in this discussion was the effect that organizational and individual decisions can have on morale and motivation.

Good decisions influence morale, trust and productivity. The decisions made by an organization's leadership team have far reaching effects on the success of the organization, the lives of individuals, and the organizational culture. Two key questions about decision making in any organization were reviewed. They were:

- What role do ethics play in decision making?
- How can ethical decision making be improved?

Thought provoking ethical questions were raised to demonstrate how ethical considerations influence decision making, and ethical principles were analyzed in the context of how they impact motivating and influencing others.

Positive interpersonal communication is critical to the success of any organization. This is especially true within organizations in which both paid staff and volunteers are essential to the successful execution of the day-to-day activities.

COMMUNICATION AND CONFLICT

A basic tenet of interpersonal communications is that each person should be willing to acknowledge and respect the other person's perspective and avoid projecting one's own motivations, ideas, understanding and interpretation of the subject on the other person.

In the previous chapters, basic communication models were introduced as they related to one-on-one communication. In this chapter the discussion will expand to include the complexity of communications between multiple parties and examine how and why communication can both cause and resolve conflict.

In all conflicts, regardless of whether they are between neighbors, friends, committee members, spouses, congregants, labor unions and management, or warring nations, the prescribed remedy to achieve peace and maintain the relationship between the parties is communication. Conflicts in which the parties want or need to mutually reach an agreement often require voices of reason to facilitate communication between the parties.

Third party intervention by someone not involved in the conflict, such as, pastors, marriage counselors, ambassadors, lawyers, mediators, arbitrators or judges is commonplace. They can help to clarify the issues, illuminate misunderstandings and reduce or resolve conflict. While some conflicts may not result in a mutually acceptable agreement, communication is the only way for the parties to exchange ideas and attempt to arrive at a peaceful resolution.

JUDGMENTAL BIASES

In the first chapter, the sender / receiver transmission model of communication was discussed. This concept describes how a message is encoded by the sender and decoded by the receiver and how it relates to two-way communication. However, oftentimes multiple parties are involved in the encoding and decoding process of communication and the original message becomes garbled. For example, think of the children's game of telephone, or of a communication workshop in which a person whispered a message in the ear of the first person and each successive person in the group whispered the message to the next person, and ultimately the final person repeated the message to the entire group. Ultimately, the final message barely resembled the original message. This is because each person decoded the message through their own inferences and judgmental biases derived from the differences in their background (culture, gender, ethnicity, ideology, life experiences, and other factors that separate us).

Communication misunderstandings can be a potential source of conflict; thus, it is important to avoid reliance upon information that may be distorted or inaccurate. Whenever distortion is likely (due to environmental noise or hearsay information), it is advisable to discuss the subject in an environment where misunderstandings are unlikely to occur. If possible, meet directly with the original source of the information. Even when the message is communicated with clarity it can still be misunderstood. This is due to judgmental biases.

JUDGMENTS, OPINIONS, AND EVALUATIONS

Oftentimes, a person allows appearance, gender or ethnicity to impede communications. Culture and ethnicity, physical attributes, gender differences, and assumptions about sex roles are all factors that influence a person's perspectives. People make assumptions about general attitudes, intelligence, competence, friendliness, rank, status, honesty, trustworthiness, and integrity primarily based upon their perspectives.

Bill Bennett, Chief Operations Officer of the McNeill Group, shared the following insights in an article titled, *"Is "JOE" Making the Decisions Which Will Produce the Best Results?"* (Bill Bennett, COO The McNeill Group 2011)

"Have you met "JOE"? We each have a "JOE" within us – actually, many "JOEs". Our view of "the way things are" is our truth. It is our paradigm, our framework for viewing the world, and it shapes our actions. Within our paradigm are Judgments, Opinions and Evaluations, or "JOEs." We form judgments about our boss, our team, our customers – about EVERYTHING. Our task is to identify our JOEs and their sometimes hidden role in our decision-making, and the key is to manage them... Are you somehow "JOE-free"? Are you completely free of Judgments, Opinions and Evaluations? It is simply human nature to have and use our JOEs to navigate our way through life. It is not a bad attribute. Without the ability to determine what is fair vs. unfair, good vs. bad, right vs. wrong, safe vs. unsafe, life would be difficult, if not impossible. So, then, JOES are good? Mostly, yes. The key is to be aware of ALL your JOEs and to determine which of them are producing the results you truly want."

We often see others through our own "JOEs." Thus, the first step to avoid misunderstandings and to develop and maintain a harmonious environment is self-awareness of our own "JOEs."

Preconceived ideas and biases can taint positive communications if the parties are not sensitive to each other's perspective concerning the topic being discussed. For example, many volunteers are utilized in agencies, organizations, and institutions that provide social services in their communities and most people have a perception about the pros, cons, costs and benefits to provide social services. Oftentimes, these perspectives are value-based and positional. Whether the issue is to provide free shelter to the homeless, condoms to prostitutes, birth control to teenagers, government funding for abortions or healthcare for the elderly, people tend to have a perspective that is biased in the direction of their own beliefs.

Judgmental biases can also be attributed to labels that one places upon another person, such as referring to a person as being "narrow-minded" because of a stance that person has taken in the past regarding a particular subject.

Oftentimes, people draw conclusions without having all of the facts pertaining to a particular decision and they decide that the subject is closed for further discussion. This is often seen during labor negotiations or during marital disputes when the parties refuse to discuss a particular subject on the basis of, "they always say no" or "they never listen."

Although we are taught not to judge, everyone has judgmental biases. These biases may cause us to reach conclusions prematurely based upon information that goes beyond our own personal sensory data.

"None of us is immune from the bias that Stanford psychologist Lee Ross calls the "fundamental attribution error." It is the tendency for observers to underestimate situational influences and overestimate dispositional influences upon behavior... We assume that people are responsible for the things that happen to them... Causal inferences are usually subconscious snap judgments made whenever we see others in action." (Griffin 1994, 142, 143)

For example, attribution errors may influence a person to assume that people on welfare are lazy, or that drug addicts choose to be addicted to drugs, or that homeless people don't want to work. These assumptions can cause conflict between family members that are dealing with these unfortunate situations.

Cognitive consistency is a person's attempt to make sense out of life experiences. People do this when they consciously avoid opposing views and rationalize life experiences that are inconsistent with their own ideas and beliefs. They may seek reassurance after making tough decisions or draw inferences based upon what they believe to be true. We all tend to view events from our own point of view. The process of drawing inferences is natural. Inferences can impact interpersonal relations because they generally draw conclusions about a person's character.

ATTRIBUTION THEORY

Social psychologist Fritz Heider, a pioneer of the concepts of social perception and causal attribution, developed the Attribution Theory. He wrote that people constantly draw inferences about why people do what they do by making personality judgments based upon observed behavior. "All our biased judgments involve a decision between personal and environmental control... We constantly assess how much an action is due to personality as opposed to environmental pressure. When judging others, our tendency is to discount external factors and put our thumb on the character side of the scale." (Griffin 1994, 141, 142) Dr. Heider defined attribution as an effort to "predict and control the world by assigning transient behavior to relatively unchanging dispositions." (Griffin 1994, 141)

Attempts to predict and control the world around us are at times justifiable and prudent. Prediction is a survival skill that helps us to assess and anticipate immediate danger. It may warn us of potentially harmful transactions or even volatile situations. Responses to another person's communication are based upon how we perceive the behavior, the intention, or the motive that we ascribe to the other person's behavior.

Attribution is a three-step process through which others are perceived:

Step 1: Perception of the action. What action was observed? How was it perceived?

Step 2: Judgment of intention. What action was intended? Did the person mean to do it or was it unintentional?

Step 3: Attribution of disposition. What action was assigned to the person's behavior versus external factors?

The ability to make causal inferences from another person's behavior is intuitive. Accurate inferences can attribute to knowing if a person might do us harm. The process of attribution can help us determine another person's disposition and propensity to demonstrate a particular behavior. This process can be helpful when we try to determine an effective method to communicate unpleasant or potentially controversial information. However, it should be noted that inaccurate inferences can cause conflict.

The attribution process is a method of systematically evaluating causes of behavior in an attempt to understand why things happen. It places an emphasis on rationality, but it fails to consider the impact that erroneous assumptions can have on relationships. Because its focus is to assign responsibility and anticipate a person's reactions based on perceptions that are influenced by internal beliefs and motivations, it tends to lead to finger pointing and laying blame on the other person.

ATTRIBUTION THEORY AND CONFLICT

In an effort to protect our values, freedoms, self-image or power position, we have a natural tendency to think that the other person is the problem. Once the cause of the conflict is attributed to the other person, then we attempt to determine why the other person is being difficult, rather than focusing on our own behavior and actions. Sometimes, personal traits are attributed to the cause of the conflict. Traits, such as, laziness, incompetence, insensitivity, aggressiveness, self-centeredness, or terms such as, "he has a chip on his shoulder" are attributed to the cause of the conflict.

Research has shown that people tend to pick personal dispositional qualities and ignore situational influences; this tendency can be the cause of many conflicts. By focusing on personality traits rather than situational factors we are able to satisfy our need for self-preservation and come to the conclusion that the other person is fully responsible for the conflict.

When we respond to conflict by placing the blame on the person's personality, the potential problem is that we may also assume that the other person is unwilling to change. As a result, the conflict may go unresolved based upon our assumption. If we are committed to the relationship then we are more likely to work to reach a resolution. If the relationship can be changed in some way, then improvements may be seen and the conflict resolved.

Effective communication and the exchange of information can reduce the number of fundamental attribution errors. Sharing information reduces the potential for attribution errors because it reduces ambiguity and it can reveal the underlying situational causes that may be at the root of the conflict. Personality attributions can cause problems as well by inviting the other person to respond with threats, name calling, screaming, and finally closing down the communications by refusing to talk. False assumptions are likely unless the parties talk to each other about the problem. Every conflict has two sides. An open dialogue and an exchange of information can provide both sides with an opportunity to own the responsibility for their actions.

Attribution Theory Conflict Resolution Questionnaire

A basic understanding of the attribution theory and the principle of fundamental attribution error can be helpful in resolving conflicts. In *Managing Interpersonal Conflict* (Donohue 1992), the authors provided the following Attribution Theory questionnaire that can aid in identifying attribution behavior during a conflict:

The purpose of this questionnaire is to see how well you understand attribution theory and its impact on conflict. Read these comments from people, describing the causes of their conflicts. Check the statements that contain attributions that are most likely to lead toward *successful* conflict resolution:
   1. _____ "Maybe our relationship can't handle this pressure."
   2. _____ "Why doesn't he stop being so stubborn about this problem?"
   3. _____ "Why didn't I tell her how I felt about her problem?"
   4. _____ "He just doesn't understand me."

5. _____ "I guess his parents made him avoid conflict too much."
6. _____ "My reaction was probably uncalled for."
7. _____ "I guess he just doesn't care about me."
8. _____ "I forced the confrontation, but he overreacted."
9. _____ "Was my timing bad in confronting this problem?"
10. _____ "I can get pretty angry at times."

If you said that statements 1, 3, 6, 9, and 10 were productive, you were right. All the others contain personality attributions that paint the wrong face on the conflict. The productive statements open opportunities for change and show flexibility in creating solutions. (Donohue 1992, 57)

The attribution theory not only describes how a person tends to attribute personality traits to dispositional behavior, it also states that a person will create expectations about future events by attempting to anticipate how the other person will react to confrontation. They will try to anticipate likely reactions as a means to predict how effective their own conflict management strategies might be. Research shows that people generally see others as more competitive than themselves; thus, they tend to overreact and overstate the other person's position.

EXAGGERATION AND CONFLICT

Exaggeration is another way to create expectations based on false assumptions. During conflict, it is common for both sides to overestimate or exaggerate the other side's position. It is natural for a person to form perceptions about what the other side believes. Exaggeration of the perceived conflict can occur when intentions, purposes, plans, goals, values, beliefs, or ideology are at the root of the controversy. When these root causes are not mutually shared or an agreement on what is best cannot be reached, then conflict can arise and the relationship may suffer. This often happens when either side becomes overly pessimistic. They give up because they believe the gap in their positions is insurmountable and that there is no common ground on which to base a resolution.

In an article written on judgmental biases in conflict resolution, the authors write, "If people hold erroneous assumptions about the gap between their own position and that of the other side, then people might decide that it is not worth even sitting down at the bargaining table on the grounds that any discussion is fruitless. The fact that we exaggerate the extent of conflict means that information exchange among parties is crucial. Unless both sides to a conflict discuss the nature of their beliefs, assumptions, and concerns, each side continues to perceive the other as unreasonable and extreme." (Thompson, Nadler and Lount 2006)

The authors concluded by stating, "Exaggeration of conflict comes in two forms: each side tends to see the other side's position as more extreme than it really is, and one's own side is also seen as more extreme than it really is." (Thompson, Nadler and Lount 2006)

PREJUDICES AND PASSIONS

Rarely is it prudent to meet prejudices and passions head-on because the parties are more apt to become positional and unwilling to listen to the other side's point of view. This is particularly true when one side views the other side as being unreasonable or narrow minded. Examples of this can be seen in debates regarding abortion, same-sex marriage, permitting teachers to carry concealed weapons in classrooms, sending jobs overseas, stem cell research, human cloning, and other potentially controversial issues. Each one of these topics or any other issue that a person is passionate about is capable of damaging relationships unless constructive communication techniques are used to guide the discussion.

One method that may be used to help to resolve philosophical differences is "The Perspective-Taking Paradigm" (Krauss and

Morsella 2006). This theory supports a collaborative effort of communication to convey emotionally sensitive information on controversial subjects. It considers the impact that a person's perspective has on resolving the conflicts. A basic assumption of this paradigm is:

> "Perspective taking assumes that individuals perceive the world from differing vantage points and that, because the experiences of each individual depend to some degree on his or her vantage point, messages must be formulated with this perspective in mind...In the best of circumstances, it is difficult to take the perspective of another accurately; the more unlike oneself the other happens to be, the more difficult the task becomes.
>
> In conflict situations, even more problematic than the absence of common ground may be the misperception of common ground—incorrect assumptions that communicators make about what their partners know. It is well established that people's estimates of what others know, believe, or value tend to be biased in the direction of their own beliefs—what they themselves know." (Krauss and Morsella 2006, 150)

The authors continue to state that there are two reasons that misperceptions are common in conflict:

1. The magnitude of the perspective differences; and,
2. The perceived differences heighten the tendency to categorize the participants as members of in-groups or out-groups.

In cases that involve judgmental biases and perceived differences in perspectives, it may be wise to engage a neutral third-party mediator that can help the parties see that their positions may not be as extreme or as different as they perceive them to be. A pastor, counselor, teacher, boss, or any third party that is neutral can help to surface "false" conflicts and misunderstandings. However, at times, it may be best to use a professional mediator or arbitrator.

Effective mediators say less and listen more. They ask open-ended questions, such as:

- Tell me more
- And what else?
- Can you tell me about the problem?
- What else can be done?
- Help me to understand why that is important to you.
- How can I help?
- What do you think is the cause?
- How would you like to solve this problem?
- What do you want, really?
- What is keeping you in this conflict?
- How can you change your reaction?
- For you, what is the real issue?

The process of asking questions and clarifying assumptions about what the other person wants or doesn't want can help the parties identify the issues. They can then pinpoint each participant's concerns and then develop a mutually agreeable solution to the problem.

GROUPTHINK

Life experiences shape a person's perspectives and over time these perspectives can shape an organization's culture. This is especially true in organizations that idolize its leader or brand. Steve Jobs, the co-founder of Apple, is an excellent example of how a person's perspectives can shape an organization's culture. When he selected his successor, many people wondered how the organization would be impacted. Would the *"groupthink"* concept guide the future decisions made at Apple? The concept of groupthink suggests that "members of a decision-making group set aside their doubts and misgivings about whatever policy is favored by the emerging consensus so as to be able to concur with other members." (I. Janis 1982) Cohesiveness is the main factor underlying the groupthink theory.

Due to the very strong "we-feeling" of solidarity at Apple and the desire to maintain relationships and the image of the brand name, Apple is a prime example of how groupthink can become the organization's culture to preserve group harmony and the legacy of Steve Jobs. Groupthink can, however, push concurrence-seeking to the point that it overrides realistic alternatives due to closed-mindedness and organizational constraints that produce less than optimal outcomes.

Irving Janis, a Yale social psychologist questioned how acknowledged groups of experts could make terrible decisions. He researched various fiascos such as, the *Challenger* disaster, the handling of the Bay of Pigs, and the Watergate break-in to determine how such grievous errors could be made by groups comprised of highly intelligent people. Based on his research, he developed the Groupthink theory. Groupthink is defined as "a mode of thinking that people engage in when they are deeply involved in a cohesive in-group, when the members' strivings for unanimity override their motivation to realistically appraise alternative courses of action." (Janis 1997)

For instance, in the case of the space shuttle *Challenger,* President Ronald Reagan appointed a presidential commission to determine the probable cause(s) of the accident. Dr. Janis reviewed the five-volume published report of the commission's findings. The testimony presented during the hearings revealed that the day prior to the launch, the engineers from Thiokol, the company responsible for the rocket booster, expressed concerns that the flight might be risky due to the fact that the "O-ring seals" on their rocket motor had never been tested in temperatures below 53 degrees Fahrenheit. NASA's managers had already postponed the launch three times. Therefore, they were fearful of negative public opinion if they postponed the launch again. Similarly, Thiokol's management team was concerned that they might lose future NASA contracts if they scrubbed the mission. The Thiokol leadership team and NASA's managers met and concurred to proceed with the launch. The presidential commission concluded that in addition to the defective O-ring seal, the decision-making process was also a contributing cause of the disaster.

Dr. Janis' research enabled him and his colleague, Leon Mann, to identify eight symptoms that can point to a groupthink mentality. They are:
1. Illusion of Invulnerability.
2. Belief in Inherent Morality of the Group.
3. Collective Rationalization.
4. Out-group Stereotypes.
5. Self-Censorship.
6. Illusion of Unanimity.
7. Direct Pressure on Dissenters.
8. Self-Appointed Mindguards. (Janis 1997, 238, 239)

In the *Challenger* example cited above, the group collectively minimized the data that did not support their decision to proceed with the launch and only listened to information that affirmed their decision. Their collective rationalization and the direct pressure on the dissenters (Thiokol's engineers) resulted in them not even asking Thiokol's expert on O-rings to give his input in the final decision. The senior leadership teams from Thiokol and NASA reached a consensus as a result of overpowering pressure from within the group to seek unanimity.

Groupthink tends to be more prevalent at the top of an organization because the senior leadership team is more insulated from outside advice. When an organization's leadership team falls victim to groupthink, open dialogues are stifled and effective decision making is impacted by incomplete information and the failure to examine alternatives. While short-term success may be achieved, there is a low probability for long-term success. Groupthink can also cause internal conflict from members of the "out-group" and impact morale.

In certain organizations, such as religious institutions, groupthink is more apt to prevail because of the tendency of its members to be concurrence-seeking and also due to their ideological aversion to conflict. While it is always best to reach mutually agreeable decisions, groupthink can result in an increase in ill-advised decisions due to the member's strong desire to be a part of the in-group.

In an organization that relies upon volunteers, groupthink can cause the volunteers to become discouraged because their input is not welcomed. The new breed of volunteers doesn't want to simply make a contribution; they want to make a difference. (McKee 2008, 24) They want to be involved and they want to be heard.

Groupthink is not always bad. On some issues, it promotes speedy and amicable decision-making. The formation of a joint communication team can be a very effective strategic tool. It can help to avoid morale issues that may be caused by internal strife between the "in-group" and the "out-group" and ensure that all parties are heard.

JOINT COMMUNICATIONS

A joint communications team shares a common goal to investigate and discuss concerns about an organization's current challenges in an effort to contribute to the creation of solutions to improve morale issues. Working together collaboratively to create messages that are intended for multiple parties increases the likelihood that the message will be communicated accurately and diplomatically. It also provides a forum for both sides to cooperatively broaden their knowledge on the issues and simultaneously diffuse false assumptions.

Barriers to joint communications are time, budget, perceptions, resistance, distractions, lack of clarity, approval processes, willingness, knowledge, experience, egos, and people's feelings. Joint communications are not one-sided, they are not ego-based, and they are not a forum for airing an organization's dirty laundry (because it may end up in the news).

Despite the barriers, joint communication is critical to the success of the organization. It empowers people to work together to resolve issues, to silence rumors, to clearly define problems, and to create long-term sustainable solutions.

Effective joint communication requires planning, open dialogue, and on-going commitment. It is hard work, but it is necessary to maintain a harmonious work environment. Working together builds trust and respect and positively impacts the organization's overall success. Upbeat joint communications are motivational and the working together process is a constructive way to effectively develop long-lasting, mutually gratifying relationships.

SUMMARY

In this chapter, the impact of judgmental biases, erroneous placement of blame on others, and the refusal to consider the other person's perspective were discussed and suggestions were provided to constructively handle these situations. The Attribution Theory was explained, including attribution errors. A questionnaire was provided to assess one's ability to determine which one of attributions would most likely lead toward constructive communications.

A section was included that described the effect that exaggeration and false assumptions can have on the escalation of conflict and how to determine the real cause of the conflict in order to find a solution. Finally, a discussion was included on the Groupthink theory that discussed how it can positively or negatively impact volunteer relations. This chapter concluded with a discussion on the benefits of developing and implementing joint communication strategies to build an atmosphere of mutual trust and respect.

Section 1 Conclusion

Cooperation begins with communication. The collective wisdom, knowledge, and experience of a broad base of people are needed to ensure the success of any organization. A team comprised of both paid staff and volunteers is ripe with potential to excel at serving its constituents; this is because the volunteers have a passion to serve and a personal interest to achieve the shared goals of the organization.

Everyone has beliefs, convictions, theories, impressions, and opinions, (both conscious and unconscious) about human motivation and behavior. These views can affect relationships (both positively and negatively) within an organization. At times, tensions arise and conflict ensues. The manner in which conflicts are resolved has a direct impact on the future of individual relationships, and possibly, the entire organization.

In the next section, "Working Together in Unity," foundational conflict management theories and principles for working together will be covered. There are various methods to handle conflicts, such as, compromising, collaborating, avoiding, withdrawing or accommodating. These methods are often used in an attempt to minimize or to avert discord in an attempt to avoid confronting the person or the issue that needs to be addressed.

The next section will offer guidance on how to constructively handle conflict and at the same time maintain the relationship. It will include discussions on the best practices for conflict resolution to maintain cooperative relationships.

SECTION 2 – WORKING TOGETHER IN UNITY

INTERACTIVE ENGAGEMENT

Life without confrontation is directionless, aimless, and passive. When unchallenged, people tend to drift, to wander or to stagnate. Confrontation is a gift. Confrontation is a necessary stimulation to jog one out of mediocrity or to prod one back from extremes. Confrontation is an art to be learned. (Augsburger 1981, 51) Many people would differ with these statements because they are afraid of confrontations. The basic fact is confrontations are inevitable, but they do not have to result in a negative outcome.

Confrontations can be described as an interactive engagement between parties that hold differing views regarding a particular subject. Confrontations can occur when there is a conflict between one's ideas, beliefs, or opinions; or between the people themselves.

Conflict resolution is a shared responsibility. At some point in everyone's life they will face conflict. Conflict is an opportunity to work together to reconcile differences. In general, people tend to feel comfortable with others who share the same views, values and attitudes. The manner in which a person or a group responds to others that do not share the same views is often the cause of the conflict. When this happens, the tendency is to either withdraw, to ignore, or to challenge the other person and attempt to change that person's point of view. In the latter case, the discussion can become a win-lose situation. A reason for this is that when people are focused on making their point and on winning, they tend to lose sight of what they have in common with each other and only see the differences.

People are often surprised at how much they have in common when they take the time to look at the situation objectively. Conflict management is a process of helping people to get past their differences by focusing on their shared interests. Everyone has a duty and an active, positive role to play to ensure that confrontations are resolved in a manner that does not permanently impair the relationship.

To be effective at conflict management, you need to have strategies that are practical; that can be applied to various situations and help the parties continue to develop good working relationships for the future. To achieve a sustainable, long-term relationship, people must learn to build trust. As stated above, confrontation is an art to be learned.

In this chapter, we will discuss successful strategies for finding common ground to deal with differences, build trust, and maintain positive and harmonious relationships. Proven methods of constructive confrontation will be explored.

ORGANIZATIONAL EMPLOYEE ENGAGEMENT

Organizations are made up of diverse members who each have their own ideas about how to accomplish a task. Each person has their own personal needs, interests and goals. They have their own style of interacting with others and they have their own standards of performance. Every interaction has the potential to produce tension and generate conflict if a person's needs, interests, or goals appear to be in opposition to those of another person or those of the organization. If the conflict is unmanaged, it has a tendency to escalate because the parties will typically take positions and polarize the issues.

Several years ago, National Public Radio reported on a story from Saint Louis where the Pro-Life and Pro-Choice groups were adamantly opposed to one another. The only thing they could initially agree on was that neither side wanted violence. The leadership teams of both organizations wanted to help pregnant women but each side held very strong, very different beliefs on how they should provide the help. However, due to their shared passion to address the rising number of unwed mothers in their community, they sought to find out if there was anything they could agree on that could become a source of common ground to address this issue. They discovered that they had a mutual interest concerning pregnant teenagers. As a result, they were able to join together to successfully create and sponsor a project to educate adolescents and to help pregnant teenagers. They avoided a win-lose situation by looking for what they had in common and they were able to jointly provide a beneficial service to the community. (Bunker 2006)

Nonprofit and religious organizations are often comprised of people that want to passionately share their beliefs about the organization's mission and purpose. Their beliefs on how the organization should operate may be steeped in tradition and grounded in history. Because of this, it is often difficult to recognize what works and what needs to be changed. However, as a new influx of employees, both volunteers and paid staff unites with the organization, they bring with them their new ideas, perspectives and attitudes. These new ideas can help the organization improve. At times, the traditionalists may want to keep things as they are and not listen to the new ideas. When this happens, conflicts can occur. One well-established business model that has been successfully used to effectively incorporate the old with the new is the Appreciative Inquiry approach.

APPRECIATIVE INQUIRY

The Appreciative Inquiry process is founded upon the principle of doing more of what has worked well in the past, rather than doing less of what has not worked. If an organization can envision the possibilities by valuing and appreciating the best of what it is, then it can create its future success through the expression of words that magnify the positive qualities of the past that will propel it into the future.

The Appreciative Inquiry approach looks for the very best experiences from the past in order to carry the best into the future and amplify it. As an example, let's consider how this approach can be used to unite and ignite a group of volunteers at a well-established nonprofit organization. The volunteers are used to augment the paid staff to successfully accomplish its mission. Let's suppose that some new volunteers join the organization but they encounter resistance when they make recommendations on how to provide food for the needy. Based on their observations, they believe there is a more effective way to provide this service. This proposed new approach will reduce the amount of time that is required for the recipients to receive the food.

The long-term volunteers have become cynical because their attempts to do things in a different manner were met with resistance. Both groups of staff share a passion for the organization and for serving those in need. They know the organization has historically been very successful and they want to be a part of the organization's future successes. The volunteer program administrator recognizes that morale is low and wants to do something that will enthuse and unite the team. She decides to try the Appreciative Inquiry approach. She wants to avoid confrontation. She has heard that rather than focus on negative experiences, the participant's share memories of past successes that can create energy and ignite enthusiasm to achieve future success.

The Appreciative Inquiry approach looks for what works in an organization. "The tangible result of the inquiry process is a series of statements that describe where the organization wants to be, based on the high moments of where they have been. Because the statements are grounded in real experience and history, people know how to repeat their success." (Hammond 1996, 7)

Studies have shown that people are very good at talking about what doesn't work when attempting to solve problems. However, reliving old problems tends to generate anxiety, frustration and at times finger-pointing. Appreciative Inquiry is a process of looking at what has worked well in the past and doing more of that. Rather than learning by focusing on the past mistakes, people learn by focusing on past successes. They are able to build on past success to gain momentum and generate ideas for future success. The first step in the Appreciative Inquiry process is to discuss assumptions.

Assumptions are a set of beliefs shared by a group that cause the group to think and act in certain ways. The Appreciative

Inquiry process starts by identifying assumptions so that misconceptions can be identified as well as the institutional truths. A downside of assumptions is that people may fail to see new data that contradicts their assumptions and thus miss an opportunity to improve their effectiveness. The following statements can be made about assumptions: (Hammond 1996, 13-15)

- Assumptions are statements or rules that explain what a group generally believes.
- Assumptions explain the context of the group's choices and behavior.
- Assumptions are usually not visible to or verbalized by the participants / members; rather they develop and exist.
- Assumptions must be made visible and discussed before anyone can be sure of the group beliefs.

The exposure of a long-held assumption that is rooted in a mindset that says "we've always done it this way" is the first step in creating an environment for change. The process of Appreciative Inquiry is founded upon the following assumptions: (Hammond 1996, 20, 21)

1. In every society, organization, or group, something works.
2. What we focus on becomes our reality.
3. Reality is created in the moment, and there are multiple realities.
4. The act of asking questions of an organization or group influences the group in some way.
5. People have more confidence and comfort to journey to the future (the unknown) when they carry forward parts of the past (the known).
6. If we carry parts of the past forward, they should be what is best about the past.
7. It is important to value differences.
8. The language we use creates our reality.

The Appreciative Inquiry process is designed to be used in a group setting that includes a cross-section of all stakeholders. The following sample questions can be used to help identify past experiences that inspired members of the organization. It is what made them feel valued or proud that they were a part of the organization: (Hammond 1996, 34)

- Describe a time when you feel the team / group performed really well. What were the circumstances during that time?
- Describe a time when you were proud to be a member of the team / group. Why were you proud?
- What do you value most about being a member of this team / group? Why?

After the responses to the aforementioned questions have been reviewed, then the participants should look for common threads of success and share the most "quotable quotes." Then the participants should create a list of the ideal state of circumstances in which the group felt they performed well. Once the list had been created, the participants can develop a symbolic, idealized, affirmative statement that describes "the best of the best" about the organization. The statement can be communicated in various formats, such as, in advertisements, on banners, on business cards, and in internal and external messages.

The Appreciative Inquiry approach enables the participants to find common themes and common threads about past successes. It can be a positive team-building tool to help people get past their differences by focusing on their collective accomplishments.

In the example above, everyone agreed that providing food to the needy in a timely, courteous, and respectful manner was a core value of the organization. Rather than focusing on how the service levels had dropped, they were able to identify what had worked well and develop strategies built upon past successes to meet the current need. As a result, the morale improved and better processes were implemented. They improved their efficiency and provided faster service to those in need. The Appreciative Inquiry approach is a great way to bring people together in a non-threatening environment to develop strategies to solve problems.

THE INTERACTION METHOD

Employee engagement is an interactive process designed to build higher levels of engagement, collaboration and commitment among the workforce. The Interaction Method and the Essential Facilitation Workshop were both developed by Interaction Associates. This is a management consulting and human resource development firm. They specialize in the design and implementation of organizational change and renewal processes (Interaction Associates 2003, 0). Two elements of their Interaction Method will be discussed as they pertain to employee engagement. The first element is the concept of shared responsibility and the second element is a collaborative attitude.

Shared responsibility is the principle that everyone in a meeting can play an active and positive role to produce meaningful results. (Interaction Associates 2003, 2-2) The Interaction Method is a facilitated approach to build understanding and agreement among people in a meeting setting. The principle of shared responsibility can be expanded across an entire organization to identify problems and to strategically develop solutions.

An organization can foster the sharing of responsibility by providing methods for its workforce to actively participate in the discussion of issues and concerns through communication channels. These channels may consist of blogs, suggestion boxes, email, online anonymous attitude surveys, or other easily accessible communication vehicles. These can be useful ways to gather information regarding the effectiveness of current policies, procedures, processes, organizational strategic direction, and the leadership team. Care should be taken to protect the confidentiality of the employees that express their concerns to avoid possible retaliation claims.

If an organization chooses to gather input from its workforce, then the organization has a responsibility to reply (either directly to the person or indirectly to the organization as a whole) and to provide specific feedback on what action will be taken in response to the ideas and suggestions. Although every idea and suggestion will not be implemented, it is important to address concerns; increase awareness of an organization's strategic goals and philosophy; and, to foster employee engagement. It also creates an atmosphere in which employees (both paid staff and volunteers) can collaboratively contribute to the resolution of problems that may affect morale.

Collaborative problem solving occurs when people are willing to work together to change a situation. The purpose of collaborative problem solving is to determine what the problem is, why it exists, and to identify solutions that everyone is willing to support. The Interaction Method outlines three phases of collaborative problem solving. (Interaction Associates 2003, Section 6-7) The three phases involve gaining key agreements on the problem, the solution, and the implementation of the agreed upon solutions. In the first phase, the perception of the problem is discussed.

During this phase the parties agree:

- We agree that a problem exists
- We agree that we are willing to work together to solve it
- We agree on the definition of the problem and where to focus our efforts
- We agree on the component parts and/or root causes of the problem

It is important that the parties involved in the problem-solving process possess a collaborative mindset. A collaborative attitude is a mindset that guides individuals to act in a cooperative and impactful manner. (Interaction Associates 2003, Section 2-2) The willingness to share ideas and brainstorm solutions is fundamental to understanding the varied perceptions of the problem in order to select the best approach to reach an agreement.

The first phase of collaborative problem solving involves gathering and clarifying information, developing alternative solutions and narrowing options. They can then select the best approach to resolve their differences and move forward with creating plans to implement the recommended changes. This is a solution to the problem that both parties are willing to support. If the parties cannot agree on the problem, then it is unlikely they will be able to agree on a solution. Therefore, it is important that each person clearly understands the problem and the meaning of each recommended solution. They need to understand how this solution relates to the problem before they can make an educated decision.

The Interaction Method is useful in large groups when a facilitated approach is needed to constructively handle conflict. Neutral facilitators with a thorough understanding of the Interaction Method are required in order to maximize success. The neutral facilitators do not participate in the content, which means their role is to capture the ideas, thoughts and suggestions of the group members. They do not generate the content themselves. They are process advocates that are trained to manage the interactive engagement between the parties.

The workshop leader will guide the discussion and help the group build understanding. They will help them navigate their way to a successful outcome. While this is similar to the Breakthrough Negotiation process which will be discussed next, the Interaction Method is designed to provide train-the-trainer instruction on the core skills of essential facilitation. This instruction will be useful within the organization on a continual basis. This method provides people with the skills and knowledge necessary to facilitate sessions that help people work together planning and implementing consensus driven decisions and new ideas.

BREAKTHROUGH NEGOTIAION

Similar to the Interaction Method, Breakthrough Negotiation is a process that provides a neutral setting where people can come together to search for common ground despite their fears and anxiety about conflict. Often people "tend to overestimate the area of conflict and underestimate the amount of common ground that exists." (Emery and Purser 1996, 142) The Breakthrough Negotiation approach to problem-solving is one example of how to bring people together to identify commonalities and to resolve conflicts in which substantive differences exist.

In the book, *Getting Past No* (Ury 1991) the author wrote about "how to bring about cooperation and sustain it in the face of the seemingly insuperable obstacles that we all encounter every day." The author developed a five-point strategy called "breakthrough negotiation" to help people win the cooperation of others that hold strongly felt differences. The purpose of this five-point strategy is to turn the confrontation into a joint problem solving exercise that results in a mutually agreeable solution that meets the needs and interests of the parties. Simply stated, the five-points are:

1. Don't react.
2. Don't argue.
3. Don't reject.
4. Don't push.
5. Don't escalate.

This practical 5-step method for negotiation can be used during any controversy to move from confrontation to cooperation. Let's briefly examine this process.

Don't React

It is natural for a person to react when confronted with a difficult situation; and, in many cases the reaction provokes a counter-reaction, this can lead to conflict that can damage long-term relationships. While confrontational reactions can and do occur in nonprofit or religious organizations, it is usually after efforts have been made to appease the other side by giving in, up to the point that concessions are no longer a viable solution. At times, conflict avoidance is the most appropriate response. However, when giving in would result in compromising core beliefs or values, then it is best to stop and think about how to proceed. Reacting prevents a person from thinking clearly and looking at the situation objectively.

In physics class we learn that "for every action, there is an equal and opposite reaction." Newton's law applies to objects, not people. Objects react; whereas, people can choose to react and they can choose not to react. "Choice is a key aspect of the internal conflicts that arise when making decisions. In the book *Choose!*, the authors state that the most powerful tool we have at our disposal is a "tool called choice." They tell us it is our "ally in the best of times" and our "resource in the most challenging times." They go on to say, "All of us are called upon to make dozens, perhaps hundreds, of choices every day. Some choices have little impact, while others have significant impact, on the direction and quality of our lives." In their book, they recognize the struggles we face every day and offer guidance on "how to make intentional and thoughtful choices, even 'on the run,' such that our lives and those around us are positively impacted."" (Adams 2010, 13)

When faced with a difficult situation, rather than react, we should step back and look at the situation objectively. Calmly evaluate the circumstances as a person on the outside looking in and look for common ground. Try to determine the underlying cause of the conflict and identify the tactics the other person is using to try to win the argument.

In *Getting Past No*, the author states, "Often you don't even realize you are reacting, because you are too enmeshed in the situation. The first task, therefore, is to recognize the tactic. In ancient mythology, calling an evil spirit by its name enabled you to ward it off. So, too, with unfair tactics—identify them and you break the spell they cast." (Ury 1991, 39) He continues by stating there are three general categories of unfair tactics that people will use during conflict: obstructive, offensive, or deceptive. Following are examples of each type of tactic:

1. <u>Obstructive</u>: Stone walls. A stone-wall tactic is a refusal to budge. The other side may try to convince you that they have no flexibility and that there is no choice other than their position. (e.g. "What's done is done." "It's company policy." "You can take it or leave it.")

2. Offensive: Attacks. Attacks are pressure tactics designed to intimidate you to make you feel so uncomfortable that you ultimately give in to the other side's demands. The attack may be a threat or a personal attack on the other person's credibility. (e.g. "You haven't been in this job long, have you?")
3. Deceptive: Tricks. Tricks are tactics to dupe you to give in. They take advantage of the fact that you assume your counterpart is acting in good faith and is telling the truth. This can be done by manipulating data, pretending to have more authority to make decisions, or making additional demands after an agreement has presumably been reached. (e.g. "This sounds good, but I have to check with the manager for approval.") (Ury 1991, 40, 41)

If you are able to recognize these tactics, you will be able to neutralize their effect and constructively move forward with resolving the dispute. It is always best to stop, think, listen and avoid making important decisions on the spot. Your own worst enemy can be your own quick reaction. Rather than react, mentally construct a mutually satisfactory way to resolve the dispute and maintain the relationship. Choose to make thoughtful choices!

Don't Argue

A common mistake that people make is to try to reason with a person that is not receptive to hearing what is being said. When a person is angry, it is unlikely that person will be willing to listen. It is best to try to understand why the person is angry rather than try to ignore it and fix the problem instead. Methods that can be used to defuse the anger are: (Ury 1991, 55-73)

- Active listening – be willing to give the other person a chance to fully express his concerns without interruptions.
- Acknowledge their point of view and their feelings. This will aid in defusing their emotions.

- Offer an apology for your actions that contributed to the dispute.
- Agree wherever you can without conceding.
- Express your views without provoking.
- Acknowledge your differences with optimism.
- Create a favorable climate for negotiation.

The aforementioned methods for defusing anger are useful aids that can be used to assess a situation while simultaneously allowing the other person to express reasons for being upset.

To turn the tide to create a positive environment, it is important to be open to new ideas, to be willing to consider alternatives, and to get the facts (albeit these facts may be based solely on the other person's point of view). This is a time to listen and to inquire. Ask open-ended questions that are geared toward establishing rapport and building trust. Withhold opinions. Create a favorable climate by showing a willingness to find a win-win solution.

Don't Reject, Don't Push, and Don't Escalate

The final three steps of the Breakthrough Negotiation process offers suggestions on how to use various communication techniques, such as reframing the question, asking clarifying questions, allowing the other side to save face, and involving a neutral third-party in the negotiation. All of these approaches have been covered in Section 1 of this book and will therefore not be repeated in this section. The ability to express the disagreement in a way that does not shut off further ideas and input from the other person is the key that will allow you to explore the reasons for the conflict and to reach a consensus on how to proceed.

Breakthrough Negotiation is a process to identify interests, develop options that will meet those interests, agree on a standard by which the options can be evaluated, consider alternatives, and reach an agreement that both sides can live with. Although only a few nonprofit or religious organizations will ever need to employ formal negotiators to help them resolve internal conflicts, understanding the process of Breakthrough Negotiation is important because it provides a systematic method of finding common ground to resolve any dispute.

EMOTION AND CONFLICT

One aspect of conflict that is apt to surface in all five steps of Breakthrough Negotiation is emotion. Managing your own emotions throughout this process is essential to transition the discussion from conflict to cooperation to consensus.

One of the most important skills a person can learn is to recognize and control emotional responses during tense situations. Emotions, such as, fear, anger, hatred, humiliation, guilt, hope, and confidence can affect conflict and they are affected by conflict. Emotions can play a constructive or destructive role in conflict resolution. For example, fear can cause a person to avoid conflict, to respond aggressively with threats or coercion, or to seek a quick resolution out of a fear of a potential future loss.

Emotion can cause a person to react without thinking, to be argumentative, to reject ideas without giving them any consideration, to push for one's own solution at all costs, or to allow the controversy to escalate to a physical confrontation or lawsuit.

When involved in a confrontation, it is best to calm your own emotions first in order to be able to think clearly and not say something that will later be regretted. Consciously decide to listen. Focus on the situation and not the other person's personality or personal traits, i.e. "she thinks she knows everything," or "she is always late." If you are involved in a dispute in which the other person is emotional, assume:

1. you don't know what the problem is;
2. you must be contributing to the problem somehow; and,
3. the problem that has surfaced is likely not the fundamental problem.

Approach the dispute by exchanging information to reduce ambiguity.

The exchange of information and self-disclosure are effective methods of integrative problem-solving because they provide better information about the cause of the conflict and encourage each party to start to think about their own contribution to the dispute, share responsibility, and then be able to begin to develop an integrative solution that both sides believe will successfully solve the problem.

If you are involved in an emotionally charged dispute, you should pause and take time to calmly examine the conflict by thinking about your own thoughts, feelings, motivations and actions that led to the conflict and that exist during the conflict. After gaining composure, ask pointed questions and actively listen to determine and understand the real, fundamental issue. Process the issues. Determine if they are:

- Interest issues?
- Needs issues?
- Values issues?
- Relational issues?
- Power issues?

When processing the issues, keep the discussion centered on the substance, facts, and evidence in order to ascertain the most critical issue in the conflict. Once the fundamental issue has surfaced, it will be easier to identify what each side really wants.

There is a danger that an interpersonal conflict will deteriorate if the parties violate one another's personal needs or interests, or if they attack the other person's self-esteem and they make no attempt to move away from these violations. However, when people focus on the issues and underlying causes of the problem and continue in dialogue about the best way to address the issues to solve the problem, then they are more likely to strengthen and reaffirm their relationship.

The process of sharing information and the development of alternative options to resolve the dispute allows each side to save face. Maintaining face preserves one's identity and self-image as being competent and trustworthy. You should never back a person into a corner with no graceful way to escape. Nor embarrass them if you intend to continue to have a positive relationship after the conflict is resolved. Emotionally driven conflict is generally caused by a difference in opinion or purpose that frustrates someone's goals, desires, or expectations. Determining why the person is frustrated will help to identify that person's interests and needs and develop options to resolve the conflict.

INAPPROPRIATE EMOTIONAL
RESPONSES TO CONFLICT

Exercising control over one's emotions can help that person avoid exhibiting the following inappropriate responses during conflict:

Defensive Responders
- Protect or justify oneself in the face of criticism, failure, or attack.
- Believes all conflict is about who is right and who is wrong.
- Their authority and position must be defended at all costs.
- Can be argumentative, persuasive, and manipulative.
- Would rather be right than be reconciled.
- Takes a "my way or the highway" stance.
- They are very positional.

Aggressive Responders
- Confrontational.
- Believes all conflict is about power.
- Conflict is an opportunity to see who is the strongest of who is in control.
- Conflict is about winning and losing – there is no middle ground.

Defensive responders and aggressive responders will both use threats and intimidation to disrupt decision-making and interfere with efforts to reconcile differences.

In nonprofit or religious organizations, defensive and aggressive responders are apt to threaten to resign if they cannot have their way. If this should happen, accept the resignation when it is offered. Threats and intimidation should be dealt with firmly and quickly. Immediately accept the resignation and advise the person that manipulative, controlling behavior is unacceptable because it destroys relationships, disrupts harmony and lowers morale. This may seem harsh and it may even seem to be an emotional response to the other person's behavior, but it is not. Boundaries must be established in every organization and people must be held accountable for their actions. Successful organizations cannot afford to retain people that repeatedly display inappropriate behavior and are unwilling to change. Conflict avoidance is never an acceptable long-term solution to maintain harmony.

Conflict avoidance is common in nonprofit or religious organizations where harmonious relationships are an expectation and people are taught to be patient and kind and to love one another. While it would be hoped that everyone would live by these guiding principles, experience has taught us that this is not the case. At times, everyone allows their emotions to impact their interactions with others.

Everyone experiences conflicts—it is a part of life. The Bible teaches that Christians can have legitimate differences of opinion on "disputable matters" (Romans 14:1) which means there will be disputes in churches and religious organizations. It is a fact of life. Having differences is not a sin. However, in the midst of conflict a person should avoid bitterness, unforgiveness, anger, slander, gossip or unwholesome talk because these responses do not aid in resolving the conflict. Rather the parties should address the issues that are causing the dispute. There are various ways to do this. Following is a list of examples that can be used to aid in the discussion as appropriate:

Open Dialogue:
- Acknowledge your own feelings and ideas about the problem.
- Admit your position.
- Acknowledge and respect the other person's perspectives.
- Own your assertions (Don't say, "Everyone thinks you…" – say what you think).
- Be clear and specific.
- Avoid exaggerations, i.e. "always," "never".
- Avoid negative criticism—do not take a "we" versus "they" or "us" versus "them" position—rather take a "we" versus "the problem" stance.

Apologize:
- A sincere and appropriately timed apology includes:
- Acknowledge and accept your role in the situation.
- Explain the problem in general terms—be accurate and truthful.
- Offer a solution to the immediate problem.
- Explain the impact of the solution.
- Choose your words carefully.

Although avoiding difficult conversations may be the easiest solution, it is never the best solution if the parties want to maintain their relationship. Disagreements are a normal part of developing and maintaining a relationship. Disagreements happen. It's how a person responds to them that determines the outcome. The aforementioned suggestions are practical ideas on how to handle difficult conversations that can aid in maintaining an environment of cooperation, mutuality and trust.

In closing, when people are focused on the common good of something they believe in, they will strive to see it succeed. While conflict in life is inevitable, it is not insurmountable. In any organization, its most valued asset is its relationship with and among its people. The success of the organization is a huge motivator to get people to sit down and work together to resolve their differences.

SUMMARY

In this chapter practical strategies have been presented that can be applied to varying situations. These strategies can help the parties involved continue to develop good working relationships for the future. Three approaches that may be used to find common ground to resolve disputes were explored. The first approach, Appreciative Inquiry, provided a method to approach problem solving in a positive, non-confrontational manner. The second approach, the Interaction Method, provided guidance on using a train-the-trainer facilitated approach to resolve problems amongst teams or groups. The third approach, Breakthrough Negotiation, provided a 5-Step method to resolve a dispute when the parties involved are confrontational.

Five barriers to cooperation are: reactions, emotions, positions, interests, and lack of trust. These barriers were addressed and strategies were provided to move the parties from confrontation to cooperation.

A common thread in resolving conflicts is to understand the real issue. Asking appropriate questions is one of the most important tools a person possesses. Questions test assumptions, invite participation, gather information, and probe for hidden agendas. Effective questions allow a person to delve past the symptoms and personal emotions to get to the root cause.

Since emotions impact how questions are asked and answered, the importance of understanding how emotions affect conflict, and how emotions are affected by conflict were discussed, and practical guidance on how to manage one's own emotions was provided.

Conflict resolution is a shared responsibility. Everyone has a duty and an active, positive role to play, to ensure the success of an organization. In the next chapter, methods of constructive confrontation will be discussed. These methods are effective in handling interfaith and intra-faith issues in a positive manner. Biblical principles on creating a collaborative, harmonious work environment will also be presented.

CONFLICT IN RELIGIOUS ORGANIZATIONS

Across all major religions – Christianity, Islam, Judaism, Buddhism and Hinduism, there is a common thread for compassion and caring for others. Core teachings of each of these religions offer lessons on living in harmony within their respective societies and often serve as a foundation for international peacemakers in their efforts to attain worldwide interfaith peace.

Peace is an inherent desire of mankind. However, peace at any cost is a very high price to pay to maintain harmony. The ability to make peace and overcome conflict is a process that is crucial to any long-term relationship. Peacemaking and peacekeeping are not the same. Peacemaking is active. It is expressed through positive, constructive actions. The peacemaker is committed to proactively understand the issue, to speak the truth in love, and to apologize or forgive, as appropriate, in order to restore and maintain the relationship. Conversely, peacekeepers are generally passive; they tend to downplay or minimize events or situations. Peacekeepers often make the problem worse by enabling or ignoring the situation in hopes that the problem will go away. Conflict avoidance is seldom a long-term solution for sustainable peace.

A person's values will often become evident during a conflict. Therefore, it is essential to understand your values and beliefs as well as those of others in order to establish cooperative relationships with those that have differing ideological or religious views from your own. This knowledge can help guide you to generate multiple alternative solutions to reach a satisfying result for all concerned and overcome religious barriers.

The purpose of this chapter is to address internal conflicts or disputes that may arise in religious organizations. The principles discussed in this chapter can be useful when working on projects that require cooperation between multiple denominations. This interfaith collaboration will help to resolve disputes that may impact your community. Therefore, it is important to touch on the topic of interfaith and intra-faith cooperation.

INTERFAITH COOPERATION

One way to begin establishing interfaith cooperation is to identify the religious values and beliefs that are held within each religion that encourage harmony and constructive conflict management. Use these beliefs as a guideline to provide a framework for a peaceful and respectful approach to achieve a shared goal. (Refer to Chapter 7 - "Blending Cultures and Worldviews" for the key tenets of the major religion's worldviews. These can be used as a starting point from which to create a framework for the establishing of interfaith cooperation).

Once an understanding of the basic tenets of each religion is determined (as they relate to ethical dilemmas, basic values, and living in peace), then it will be necessary to identify a spokesperson for each religious group. Begin by identifying the religious leaders, groups, organizations and institutions that will be directly impacted by the proposed action. Who will be needed to successfully achieve the shared goal? Offer to confer in order to jointly discuss the ways to mitigate the outcome of the decision for each party. During the meeting:

- Identify each party's positions, interests and needs.
- Jointly agree to promote and reinforce principles of respect, cooperation, compassion and peacemaking. These are key elements that are contained within each religion's core teachings, beliefs and traditions.
- Adopt new ways to manage constructive relationships between the parties and to handle disputes when they arise in the future—establish a network of interfaith / intra-faith connections.
- Adhere to the universal principles of dignity, liberty, equality, justice, peace and brotherhood to establish respectful relationships.

People are more likely to work together to achieve a shared goal if their personal identity and basic values are not being compromised. Reaching an agreement on the above guidelines will help each party remain open-minded and cooperative throughout the discussions. The goal of these discussions is not to reach an either / or agreement—it is to reach a win-win agreement that every party can support.

INTRA-FAITH CONTROVERSIES

The dilemma of intra-faith controversies is that a majority of the members within the given religion hold similar values and beliefs. They tend to disagree on the interpretation of their beliefs. This is based upon various doctrines, commentaries, expositions, books and other interpretive works that attempt to explain the fundamental, foundational truths of their religion. For example, all Christians believe that Jesus is coming back to claim His followers but they do not all agree on the timing of that occurrence.

There are numerous "end times" or "last things" views that are generally accepted: Pre-millennial Pre-tribulation View; Pre-millennial Post-tribulation view; Pre-millennial Mid-tribulation view; and, Pre-millennial Pre-tribulation Partial Rapture view; Pre-millennial Pre-wrath Rapture View; Evangelical Post-Millennial view; St. Augustine's Amillennial view; and, A Second Amillennial view. While these various views may be an interesting subject for debates, it is probably not reasonable for this topic to become a cause of major dissension since no one can know the final outcome until it happens. In this case it's safe to "agree to disagree" and move on. There are other doctrinal topics that are not as easy to resolve.

An example of an ongoing intra-faith controversy is the difference in beliefs pertaining to the offices of the five-fold ministry. In the *Holy Bible,* in Ephesians it states, "So Christ himself gave the apostles, the prophets, the evangelists, the pastors and teachers, [12]to equip his people for works of service, so that the body of Christ may be built up [13]until we all reach unity in the faith and in the knowledge of the Son of God and become mature, attaining to the whole measure of the fullness of Christ." (Ephesians 4:11-13 NIV)

In August 2011, the New Apostolic Reformation (NAR) became the media's national topic of discussion because of their beliefs concerning the office of the apostle and the prophet. Most of traditional Christianity accepts evangelists, pastors, and teachers, but they do not believe in modern-day apostles and prophets. As such, members of the traditional denominations of Christianity accused the NAR of teaching false doctrines concerning apostolic governance and their belief that God still calls apostles and prophets today.

In response to the allegations that the NAR was teaching false doctrine and to statements that labeled it as a "cult," Dr. Peter Wagner, Ph.D., wrote a detailed letter on August 18, 2011 (Wagner 2011) in which he described the origins of the title "New Apostolic Reformation" and he addressed the concerns expressed pertaining to the NAR. In his letter he wrote, in part,

> Apostolic Governance. As I mentioned before, this is probably the most radical change. I take literally St. Paul's words that Jesus, at His ascension into heaven, "gave some to be apostles, some prophets, some evangelists, and some pastors and teachers for the equipping of the saints for the work of ministry" (Ephesians 4:11-12). Most of traditional Christianity accepts evangelists, pastors, and teachers, but not apostles and prophets. I think that all five are given to be active in churches today. In fact, St. Paul goes on to say, "And God has appointed these in the church: first apostles, second prophets, third teachers…" (1 Corinthians 12:28). This does not describe a hierarchy, but a divine order. Apostles are first in that order.

> I strongly object to journalists using the adjective "self-appointed" or "self-declared" when referring to apostles. No true apostle is self-appointed. First of all, they are gifted by God for that ministry. Secondly, the gift and its fruit are recognized by peers and the apostle is "set in" or

"commissioned" to the office of apostle by other respected and qualified leaders.

In the case of the NAR, much of the debate has taken place in the media. With the advent of 21st Century technology and the worldwide usage of the internet and blogs to express our views, conflict management has become even more dynamic. The parties are able to voice their views to a worldwide audience. These views can cause dissension and be very destructive if they are not responded to properly. Following are some suggestions on how to handle detrimental blogs or negative media reports if you don't have a Public Relations team to handle the crisis:

- Listen first then act.
- Acknowledge the problem.
- Authenticity is crucial—be honest and transparent.
- Educate your constituents so they can provide unified support.
- Launch/Update your blog, social media networking cites and website.
- If possible and practical, schedule media appearances.
- Exhibit love, patience, and self-control.
- Be humble.
- Maintain your dignity.
- Pray continuously and enlist the help of intercessors.

These principles will help you weather the storm and silence the media "sound bites." After enduring the initial phase of turmoil, then it will be time to adhere to more traditional methods of conflict resolution, such as, convene meetings with the dissenters to discuss positions, interests and needs and establish protocols similar to those listed for interfaith conflicts.

Fortunately, in most cases, the internet or the media will not be a conduit for the conflict to be aired. The process to handle intra-faith controversies will be similar to the process to handle interfaith conflicts. Because the majority of intra-faith members hold the same fundamental values and beliefs, the interdependence between the intra-faith denominations can be a cornerstone to establish harmonious relationships.

INTERDEPENDENCE

In the book, *Managing Interpersonal Conflict,* (Donohue 1992) the authors define conflict as, "a situation in which interdependent people express (manifest or latent) differences in satisfying their individual needs and interests, and they experience interference from each other in accomplishing these goals." The authors go on to say that, "conflict requires interdependence, and more important, it often promotes interdependence." This is because people need each other's resources, whether it's time, money or emotional support to satisfy their individual needs and interests.

Everybody needs someone else to survive. People were created to have relationships with other people. No matter how isolated a person may be or how remote the location where he or she lives, there is some system of interdependent reliance. It may be through trading, bartering, or buying food, supplies, or weapons that are necessary for survival. Interpersonal conflict arises when someone hinders another from attaining their individual needs and interests.

A link of some kind must exist between the conflicting parties for conflict to be present. If people decide they can no longer get what they want from each other, then they may decide to terminate the relationship and end their interdependence. For example, think of a conflict that has occurred at a church between the pastor and one or more of the congregants. If the congregants decide to leave and go to another church, then the relationship is severed and that conflict no longer exists. The effects of that conflict may linger for awhile, but the actual combatants are no longer engaged in the controversy.

The belief that conflict must be avoided is a common misperception that is held by many on how to solve problems in both religious and secular organizations. In churches, members will often choose to go to another church rather than to work through the conflict and experience the positive results and bonding which may be the outcome of resolving the dispute. Volunteers may become disengaged and return to just sitting in the pews.

Avoiding conflict and pretending the problem will go away on its own increases tensions and fuels the flame for sudden, emotionally charged reactions to the situation. Things such as, tears, anger, or unhealthy silence can lead to rage and destructive behavior. Conflict management is a better choice than conflict avoidance.

One definition of conflict management is, "the process of influencing the activities and attitudes of an individual or group in the midst of disagreement, tensions, and behavioral actions which are threatening the relationship and or the accomplishment of goals." (Shawchuck 1983, 21) This definition captures the interdependency that exists and the potential deterioration of the relationship that may occur, when people are unable to successfully progress toward their desired goals. When conflict is managed efficiently, some modification in role definition generally occurs that enhances and unifies the relationship.

Unity is one of the goals of the local church. Unity is the presence of genuine harmony, understanding and goodwill. Unity does not mean uniformity. It does mean blending together to resolve differences. People can have legitimate differences of opinions on "disputable matters" (Romans 14:1). Disputes over limited resources, such as, whether to spend church funds on new robes or a parking lot, can be an example of a legitimate difference. Disputes over character, lifestyles, or family values are also matters that can cause dissension in a church. When differences arise, they need to be reconciled. Various modes of handling conflicts will surface, such as, competing, compromising, collaborating, avoiding, withdrawing or accommodating. In any given situation, any one of these modes may be the best short-term choice, given the circumstances. However, over time, people are seldom satisfied with any approach that does not address the issue.

In *The Peacemaker: A Biblical Guide to Resolving Personal Conflict* (Sande 2004), the author states that there are four primary causes of conflict:

1. Poor communication.
2. Differences in values, goals, gifts, callings, priorities, expectations, interests or opinions.
3. Competition over limited resources, such as time or money.
4. Sinful attitudes, sinful behaviors, or sinful habits.

Although the term 'conflict' is an emotional word that usually generates feelings of anxiety; not all conflict is bad. A misunderstanding that results from poor communications is an opportunity for a person to choose to let it go, or to respond in haste. Oftentimes, people react to what they heard or what they think they heard without asking clarifying questions. In Scriptures we read, "A fool shows his annoyance at once, but a prudent man overlooks an insult" (Proverbs 12:16 NIV).

Asking clarifying questions, such as, "Are you saying...", "Tell me more about...", or, "Please give me an example", can help to eliminate confusion and avoid conflicts. A communication misunderstanding can also result from language barriers or cultural differences. At times, people allow frustration caused by difficulty in understanding another person's accent to cause conflict and disrupt harmonious relationships. Patience, mercy, and being humble can prevent a person from showing annoyance and allow that person to overlook a perceived insult.

SUBMISSION TO AUTHORITY

Effective leadership is the key to making peace. One underlying problem related to many issues in churches and religious organizations has to do with submission to authority. Until this issue is addressed, the problem will continue to resurface. Many interpersonal disputes and conflicts within a church are symptoms of deeper problems involving lordship and leadership. The manner in which the leadership responds to the conflict determines if, how, and when the conflict is reconciled.

At times, personal goals reign supreme and the person becomes aggressive, abusive, domineering, and uncooperative. The leadership team members in a church are the peacemakers. "Peacemaking is active and proactive. The peacemaker is committed to speaking the truth in love, to repenting, forgiving, and restoring. This is a biblical, redemptive response to conflict." (Van Yperen 2002, 172) Church leaders should actively and proactively address sinful behavior. Submission to a process of change guided by God's Word, Holy Spirit and the church will establish boundaries for accountability and encourage long lasting, life changing results.

The actions of a peacemaker are intended to restore the church member to fellowship. Any action that is taken should be handled gently and in love. Discipline and restitution should be beneficial, purposeful and encourage the church member to change. Confession and forgiveness are just the first steps to restoration. Restoration is a two-part process. It requires the peacemakers at the local church to speak the truth in love and avoid all feelings of superiority, indignation, condemnation, bitterness or resentment. And it requires: repentance, self-examination, confession, personal change and asking for forgiveness from the person that committed the wrongful act.

The purpose of asking for forgiveness is to earnestly repair the damage caused by the inappropriate conduct and to seek genuine peace and reconciliation. The person that wronged another is required to honestly admit to his or her contribution to the conflict;

not, as a means to comfort oneself, but to minister to the person(s) that was harmed. The ultimate goal for all parties involved is to forgive as God has forgiven – unconditionally and totally.

The manner in which a person handles disagreements distinguishes the level of assertiveness (instigating) from the level of cooperation (peacemaking) that will emerge during a dispute. Thoughtful word selection defuses conflict and fosters an atmosphere of cooperation.

According to the author of *Making Peace: A Guide to Overcoming Church Conflict* (Van Yperen 2002, 24), church conflict: 1) is always theological; never merely interpersonal; and, 2) is always about leadership, character, and community. The author's research concluded that, church conflicts are always theological because at the core, the disputes focus on who God is and what God requires of His people. (Van Yperen 2002, 43)

Many churches look and act like the world around them and thus conflict arises when worldviews, cultures and theology collide. The interrelationship between these external and internal influences can be seen in the decisions made by the church leaders and they may create an atmosphere of conflict if the church member's views on how to integrate these societal and theological powers within the church differ from the church leaders.

COALITIONS

Oftentimes, coalitions form when several people hold different views on how to adapt to changes within their church or organization. People are likely to form coalitions when they anticipate or experience conflict that relates to their values. As conflict develops, people are inclined to choose sides. They form coalitions because they know there is power in numbers and they know they cannot achieve their desired goals alone. Coalitions represent a single, more significant voice that the opposing leadership team must listen to. Although coalitions are generally a temporary alignment or union between two or more groups, if the coalition is successful in attaining its desired goals, then the relationships between its members tend to become permanent and they will generally remain a united force to contend with in the future to maintain their shared values.

Because coalitions are influential and power is often redefined at the end of the dispute, it is important to understand the dynamics of coalitions and to form alliances with power-brokers. One dynamic of a successful coalition is its ability to attract members from the other less successful coalitions at the end of the dispute; thus, further polarizing the parties. Post-conflict is a good time to clarify the positions, needs and interests of the opposing factions and find workable areas where each side can unite and improve relationships that may have been damaged during the conflict. This may be a good time to attend a team-building workshop or retreat to mend and strengthen relationships and to resolve fundamental differences.

IT'S ALL ABOUT ME

Western societies tend to emphasize personal rights. This tendency to focus on "me" can cause a church to lose sight of the primary focus of the church. Oftentimes, a church will seek to negotiate internal peace without reconciling fundamental differences. An example of this can be seen in how many churches have responded to the introduction of contemporary worship music into church services. Some churches have elected to have two different times for service: one that offers contemporary worship music and another which offers a more traditional service. Other churches have elected to rotate the worship teams and assign them to specific weeks of the month to lead the worship, in order to maintain peace. While both of these options provide a workable solution to this problem, they fail to address the underlying problem of making worship a matter of individual choice and personal preference rather than submitting the worship to the direction of Holy Spirit.

Once a church begins to function to satisfy individual choices and preferences, then individuality may become a focal point of ministry and of the volunteer efforts of its members. When this happens, churches can begin to suffer from "Spiritual Deficit Disorder" (Van Yperen 2002, 29) which can be described by the following symptoms:

- Individuality vs. mutuality
- Trusting self vs. trusting God
- Molding God into our image vs. molding ourselves in God's image
- Church-centered worship vs. God-centered worship

An awareness of one's uniqueness and one's God-given gifts and capabilities is not the fundamental issue; it's how a person expresses that uniqueness to attain a desired outcome. History shows that throughout the ages outstanding leaders have had a clear understanding of their own identity and that can be a positive motivator in striving for success. However, a church is a community not a competition. In the case above, the contemporary church and the traditional church should strive to maintain equilibrium between the two groups. Neither group can remain rigid in its thinking. They must find creative solutions that foster cooperative team ministry that blends the old with the new while maintaining the principles of fellowship and community upon which the church was established. Ultimately, all efforts should be judged in relationship to their eternal effects.

MEDIATION

At times, a third-party, impartial mediator may be required to engage both parties in managing the conflict. The role of the mediator is to: (Borisoff and Victor 1989)

- Deemphasize status and power differences between the parties.
- Empower both sides to explore creative solutions.
- Allow both sides to fully articulate goals, needs, concerns and interests.

- Encourage the parties to reach a mutually acceptable settlement.

A component of the settlement may be to tell the truth. Open, honest communications can minimize misunderstandings, strife and conflict. Conflict is often caused by ambiguity, implied criticism, gossip or slander. When a person is able to separate the deed from the doer then that person will be capable of moving from confrontation to cooperation.

The following is a list of conflict resolution principles, taken in part from *Communication and Conflict Management in Churches and Christian Organizations* (Gangel and Canine 1992) and it can be utilized prior to, during and after any dispute to achieve harmony:

1. Keep working on communication skills constantly.
2. Formulate a common purpose, shared vision, and mission statement.
3. Establish clear, realistic, communicable goals and objectives. Avoid ambiguity.
4. Strive to maintain harmony, unity, like-mindedness and a positive attitude.
5. Listen!
6. Establish quality control measurements. Expect excellence.
7. Evaluate performance. Provide ongoing feedback.
8. Discern hidden agendas.
9. Clearly define roles.
10. Speak the truth in love.
11. Caringly confront.
12. Separate the people from the problem.
13. Seek win-win solutions. Work together to create options that satisfy both parties.
14. Never compromise values, ethics, or biblical truths to settle a dispute.
15. Alleviate stress.
16. Celebrate success!

Disagreements are a normal part of developing and maintaining relationships. Conveying a cooperative attitude and demonstrating effective communications skills are required to become an empathetic, open-minded, cooperative communicator.

SUMMARY

The key concepts of this chapter can by summarized in this way:

"Since God has so generously let us in on what he is doing, we're not about to throw up our hands and walk off the job just because we run into occasional hard times. We refuse to wear masks and play games. We don't maneuver and manipulate behind the scenes. And we don't twist God's Word to suit ourselves. Rather, we keep everything we do and say out in the open, the whole truth on display, so that those who want to can see and judge for themselves in the presence of God. . . .So we're not giving up. How could we! Even though on the outside it often looks like things are falling apart on us, on the inside, where God is making new life, not a day goes by without his unfolding grace. These hard times are small potatoes compared to the coming good times, the lavish celebration prepared for us. There's far more here than meets the eye. The things we see now are here today, gone tomorrow. But the things we can't see now will last forever" (2 Corinthians 4:1-2; 16-18, MSG (Peterson 2002)

In conclusion, disagreements happen, but relationships and churches should not be destroyed by them. Peace and harmony can be achieved by working together to resolve differences.

BLENDING CULTURES AND WORLDVIEWS

The world is not flat – globalization, internationalism, societal cultures and divergence have forced leaders in all walks of society, including volunteer program administrators and volunteer managers, to identify key issues of concern. By addressing cultural sensitivity you can enrich your organization and embrace the diversity of our globalized settings.

Culturally, there are differences in communication practices, traditions, and thought processes. By understanding cultures and worldviews, you can learn how to recognize any unconscious tendencies you may have. We often interpret and judge other people based upon the values of your own culture and worldview. Developing interpersonal relationship skills can reduce possible tensions that may arise.

The goal of this chapter is to provide a basic understanding of six major worldviews that influence more than 3 billion people worldwide. This information can help you to establish trusting relationships and network connections across the mosaic of subcultures. These subcultures exist within organizations and institutions creating difficult challenges to achieving a common goal. Understanding these worldviews will help you to establish the connections and the relationships that are necessary for a unified front and team cooperation for the benefit of all.

WHAT IS CULTURE?

Culture has been described in many ways. There is no "universal" definition; however, the following definitions capture the essential characteristics of culture. One of the earliest definitions published in 1871 by anthropologist Edward Tylor defined culture as, "that complex whole which includes knowledge, belief, art, morals, law, custom, and other capabilities acquired by a man as a member of society." (Tylor 2005, 91) Another definition written by Geert Hofstede, an expert on international differences in work related values, stated that culture is "the collective programming of the mind which distinguishes the members of one human group from another . . . Culture, in this sense, includes systems of values; and values are among the building blocks of culture." (Hofstede 2005, 91)

Values are abstract ideas that form the bedrock of a culture, while norms are the principles or rules that people are expected to observe, they govern how people treat one another. Values include our beliefs and attitudes about concepts such as individual freedom, democracy, truth, justice, honesty, loyalty, and so on. People are willing to argue, fight and even die over values; whereas, a violation of norms usually does not cause major conflict. Some examples of norms in a workplace include: appropriate dress codes for the situation, good social manners, common courtesies, neighborly behavior, arriving on time, and maintaining order and cleanliness. A violation of these types of norms may be considered rude or ill-mannered but usually do not result in long-lasting dissension or a permanently damaged relationship.

The American Heritage College dictionary (The American Heritage College Dictionary, Fourth Edition 2007) defines culture as, "The totality of socially transmitted behavior patterns, arts, beliefs, institutions, and all other products of human work and thoughts." Thus culture refers to the whole way of life for the members of a society or group. It includes dress, customs, foods, language, family life, arts, entertainment, business transactions, education, religion and social interactions. To fully understand a culture, it should be viewed in terms of its own meanings and values, not from your own cultural perspective.

Culture and worldviews can have a powerful affect on work ethics and employment practices (such as prayer in the workplace). Volunteer program administrators and organizational leadership team members can improve their organizational environment through better understanding of these highly important factors.

Cross-cultural awareness is imperative for international organizations that recruit/attract international applicants and volunteers. This knowledge provides an insurance policy if you will, that ensures the international organization will maintain certain values that transcend those associated with the host society where the business or institution happens to be headquartered. When an organizational culture aligns with the values of the underpinning societal structure/culture, then there is cultural consistency and support of societal values.

IMPACT OF WORLDVIEWS

A person's worldview is portrayed best by that person's own words and actions. "A worldview is a commitment, a fundamental orientation of the heart, that can be expressed as a story or in a set of presuppositions (assumptions which may be true, partially true or entirely false) that we hold (consciously or subconsciously, consistently or inconsistently) about the basic constitution of reality, and that provides the foundation on which we live and move and have our being." (Sire 2009, 20)

In *The Universe Next Door* (Sire 2009) the author provides a concise introduction into major worldviews including the following in part: Christian theism, eastern pantheistic monism, and Islamic theism. The author asks eight questions to analyze each of these major worldviews. One of the questions is "How do we know what is right and wrong?" This question and its answers reveal the variety of ways that intellectual commitments are worked out in individual's lives.

The question of right and wrong is rooted in a person's religious beliefs and ethical system. Following is a brief summary of religion and ethical systems that will guide our discussion in the current chapter:

"Religion may be defined as a system of shared beliefs and rituals that are concerned with the realm of the sacred. Ethical systems refer to a set of moral principles, or values, that are used to guide and shape behavior. Most of the world's ethical systems are the product of religion. Thus, we can talk about Christian ethics and Islamic ethics. However, there is a major exception to the principle that ethical systems are grounded in religion. Confucianism and Confucian ethics influence behavior and shape culture in parts of Asia, yet it is incorrect to characterize Confucianism as a religion.

The relationship between religion, ethics and society is subtle and complex. While there are thousands of religions in the world today, in terms of numbers of adherents four dominate—Christianity with 1.7 billion adherents, Islam with 1 billion adherents, Hinduism with 750 million adherents (primarily in India), and Buddhism with 350 million adherents. Although many other religions have an important influence in certain parts of the modern world (for example, Judaism, which has 18 million adherents), their numbers pale in comparison with these dominant religions (however, as the precursor of both Christianity and Islam, Judaism has an indirect influence that goes beyond its numbers)." (Hill 2005, 98)

The subtle, yet complex implications that religion and ethics have on shaping attitudes toward work and volunteerism must be understood because they have a direct impact on an organization's culture.

In this chapter, we will be discussing each of the major religious worldviews including: Christianity, Islam, Judaism, Buddhism, Hinduism and the philosophy of Confucianism. These worldviews impact a substantial portion of the world. We will also explore the basic tenets and the response to the question, "How do we know what is right and wrong?" The responses will highlight the importance of seeing your own worldview not only within the context of vastly different worldviews but within the community of your own belief system.

What is the underlying cause for conflict with others who do not share our same point of view? A basic understanding of the various perspectives on "what is right" and "what is wrong" may give us valuable insight regarding how people process these two different concepts.

This chapter objectively states the overarching teachings found in the major religions in the world and their respective worldviews. It does not include the extreme conduct and views held by the radical "fundamentalists" that can be found in any religion. The vast majority of adherents to all major religions repudiates violence and embraces the principles of peace and justice that are found in each of their respective teachings.

CHRISTIAN WORLDVIEW

Christianity is the most widely practiced religion in the world. Approximately 20 percent of the world's people identify themselves as Christians. (Hill 2005, 98) There are three major groups of Christianity: the Roman Catholic Church, the Orthodox Church, and the Protestant Churches. A fundamental principle of the Protestant Churches is their belief in the right to individual religious freedom and the freedom to develop their own personal relationship with God. Some sociologists believe that the Protestant emphasis on individual religious freedom paved the way for modern-day economic and political freedoms and the development of individualism as an economic and political philosophy.

In 1904, a prominent sociologist, Max Weber, made note of the relationship between Protestant ethics and the emergence of modern capitalism by stating:

Business leaders and owners of capital, as well as the higher grades of skilled labor, and even more the higher technically and commercially trained personnel of modern enterprises, are overwhelmingly Protestant. (Hill 2005, 100)

According to Weber the Protestant ethics emphasize the importance of hard work, wealth creation, investment in the expansion of capitalist enterprises, and frugality. He states that these ethics paved the way for the development of capitalism in Western Europe and eventually in the United States. While this generalization does not reflect all of Christianity, it does provide some insight concerning the relationship between work ethics, individualism and reinvesting into the community which are core values for many volunteers.

A person that holds a Christian worldview believes that God transcends all things; God is infinite; and God is the creator of everything. Christianity is founded on the gospel of the Lord and Savior Jesus Christ of Nazareth. He is the one and only begotten son of God through whom all that confess and believe that Jesus is the son of God will have eternal life. When He returns He will establish the visible kingdom of God here on earth. In accordance with the gospel, forgiveness and eternal life are gifts of God's grace through faith in Christ Jesus and are freely available to all people.

God in whom all reason, all goodness, all hope, all love, all reality, and all existence has its origin is the only true and living God. There is a deep, personal dimension involved in grasping and living within the Christian worldview. "To be a Christian theist is not just to have an intellectual worldview; it is to be personally committed to the infinite-personal Lord of the universe." (Sire 2009, 286)

In response to the question, "How do we know what is right and what is wrong? the author wrote, "Ethics is transcendent and is based on the character of God as good (holy and loving)." (Sire 2009, 42) He goes on by saying Christians believe "God himself— his character of goodness (holiness and love)—is the standard. Furthermore, Christians and Jews hold that God has revealed His standard in the various laws and principles expressed in the *Holy Bible*. The Ten Commandments (listed below) are the most widely known God-given laws that guide both Christianity and Judaism:

1. You shall have no other gods before me.
2. You shall not make for yourself an idol.
3. You shall not misuse the name of the Lord your God.
4. Remember the Sabbath day by keeping it holy.

5. Honor your father and your mother.
6. You shall not murder.
7. You shall not commit adultery.
8. You shall not steal.
9. You shall not give false testimony.
10. You shall not covet.

Other foundational biblical teachings include the Sermon on the Mount, the apostle Paul's ethical teaching, the books of Psalms and Proverbs, and many other biblical passages that express God's character. Thus, for many Christians *the Holy Bible* is the absolute standard by which all moral and ethical judgments are measured.

ISLAM WORLDVIEW

With 1 billion adherents, Islam is the second largest world religion. Adherents of Islam are referred to as Muslims. Muslims constitute a majority in more than 35 countries in Africa, Asia and the Middle East. Like Christianity and Judaism, Islam in a monotheistic religion (belief in one god). "The central principle of Islam is that there is but the one true omnipotent God. Islam requires unconditional acceptance of the uniqueness, power, and, authority of God and the understanding that the objective of life is to fulfill the dictates of his will in the hope of admission to paradise." (Hill 2005, 100)

The Muslim lives in a social structure that is governed by Islamic law (as set down in the *Koran*, the bible of Islam) and shaped by Islamic values and norms of moral conduct. Some of the major tenets of Islam include (Hill 2005, 101):
1. Honoring and respecting parents.
2. Respecting the rights of others.
3. Being generous but not a squanderer.
4. Avoiding killing except for justifiable causes.
5. Not committing adultery.
6. Dealing justly and equitably with others.
7. Being of pure heart and mind.

8. Safeguarding the possessions of orphans.
9. Being humble and unpretentious.

There are many similarities in the above list with the Ten Commandments and other guiding principles found in the Holy Scriptures for Christianity and Judaism alike. They can provide a common ground for maintaining harmony to achieve a shared goal.

It should be noted that the orthodox Muslim ritual requires prayer five times a day; it requires women to be dressed in a certain manner; and it forbids the consumption of pork and alcohol. An organization or institution should consider making reasonable accommodations to provide for an inclusive, yet unobtrusive work environment.

Muslim countries that are not run by fundamentalists favor market-based systems and are receptive to foreign businesses in their country, as long as the foreigners behave in a manner consistent with Islamic ethics. One economic principle of Islam prohibits payment or receipt of interest, which is considered usury. Thus, in nations such as Pakistan, interest is illegal. "In Muslim countries, it is fine to earn a profit, so long as that profit is justly earned and not based on the exploitation of others for one's own advantage…Furthermore, Islam stresses the importance of living up to contractual obligations, of keeping one's word, and of abstaining from deception." (Hill 2005, 102)

A basic understanding of Islamic values and religious requirements will equip volunteer program administrators and the organizational leadership team with the information they need to develop the best policies and practices for Islamic staff members in the workplace.

JUDAISM WORLDVIEW

Judaism is a precursor to Christianity and Islam. Although it only has approximately 18 million adherents its influence goes well beyond its numbers. Judaism is also a monotheistic religion. The response to the question, "How do we know what is right and

113

what is wrong?" can be found in the law of Moses (including the Ten Commandments listed above), the *Torah* (the bible of Judaism), the sacred writings of the prophets and in the other laws and regulations contained in the *Torah* and other writings. Following are a brief list of social responsibility laws and regulations taken from the book of Exodus. They are similar to those found in Islamic teachings and identical to Christianity since the first five books of *the Holy Bible* are identical to the *Torah*: (Exodus 22:21-23:9) (The Holy Bible, New International Version 1984)

1. Do not take advantage of a widow or an orphan.
2. If you lend money to one of my needy people among you who is needy, do not be like a moneylender; charge him no interest.
3. Do not blaspheme God or curse the ruler of your people.
4. Do not hold back offerings.
5. Do not spread false reports.
6. Do not follow the crowd in doing wrong.
7. Do not deny justice to your poor people in their lawsuits.
8. Do not accept a bribe.
9. Do not oppress an alien, you yourselves know how it feels to be aliens, because you were aliens in Egypt.

Judaism, Islam and Christianity all have laws that require social responsibility. The concept of fairness and the requirement to provide care and assistance for the poor and needy are core tenets for each of these religions. Fairness and helping others are also primary concerns for volunteers at religious organizations and many other non-profit institutions. Thus, policies, procedures and work rules that support these ethical principles will foster harmony and cooperation in the workplace.

HINDUISM WORLDVIEW

Hinduism is the world's oldest major religion. Unlike Christianity, Judaism and Islam, it does not have an officially sanctioned sacred book such as *the Holy Bible*, the *Torah*, or the *Koran*. About 80 percent of India's population regard themselves as Hindus. There are more than 750 million Hindus worldwide making it the third largest religion after Christianity and Islam.

"Hindus believe that a moral force in society requires the acceptance of certain responsibilities, called *dharma*. Hindus believe in reincarnation or rebirth into a different body after death. Hindus also believe in *karma,* the spiritual progression of each person's soul." (Hill 2005, 102) Karma is the divine law of cause and effect by which a person's every thought, word and deed returns to that person in this or a future life. Hindus are taught to be compassionate, knowing that each experience, good or bad, is the self-created result of prior expressions of free will. "A person's karma is affected by the way he or she lives. By perfecting the soul in each new life, Hindus believe that an individual can eventually achieve *nirvana,* a state of complete spiritual perfection . . . Many Hindus believe that the way to achieve nirvana is to lead a severe ascetic lifestyle of material and physical self-denial." (Hill 2005, 102, 103)

Although Hinduism does not have a unified system of beliefs and ideas, there are some basic tenets to which they adhere to, in general. The "10 Disciplines of Hinduism" as summarized by Dr. Gangadhar Choudhury (Das 1999) include:

1. Truth
2. Non-violence
3. Celibacy, non-adultery
4. No desire to possess or steal
5. Non-corrupt
6. Cleanliness
7. Contentment
8. Reading of scriptures
9. Austerity, perseverance, penance
10. Regular prayers

The response to the question, "How do we know what is right and what is wrong?" can be found in the moral ideals in Hinduism that require a lifestyle of non-violence, truthfulness, friendship, compassion, fortitude, self-control, purity and austerity in a Hindus' quest to achieve the ultimate goal of nirvana.

Traditional Hindu values emphasize that individuals should be judged by their spiritual achievements, rather than the material accomplishments. However, since the caste system was abolished in India in the mid-20th Century, modern-day India has become a hard-working entrepreneurial society that provides more opportunities for its citizens to attain positions of responsibility and influence in their country. This new found freedom opened the door for an increase in immigration from India for its people who were once bound by the caste system. Thus, more Hindus are in the workplace as both employees and volunteers. Therefore, it is important for volunteer program administrators and organizational leadership teams to structure reward systems that fulfill their spiritual yearnings, (which can be done by providing volunteer opportunities to assist the poor and needy or caring for animals) in addition to meeting their material needs.

BUDDHISM WORLDVIEW

Buddhism was founded in India in the sixth century B.C. by Siddhartha Gautama. He was an Indian prince who achieved nirvana and became known as the Buddha (which means "the awakened one"). Today Buddhism has about 350 million followers found mostly in Central and Southeast Asia, China, Korea and Japan. Similar to Hinduism, nirvana is the ultimate goal of Buddhism. To achieve nirvana, Buddhist followers must follow the "Noble Eightfold Path" as set forth by the Buddha. The eight steps on the Noble Eightfold Path provide a practical guide to ethics, mental rehabilitation and mental reconditioning. (Fundamental Buddhism 1997) The eight steps are:
1. Right understanding.
2. Right thought.
3. Right speech.
4. Right action.

5. Right livelihood.
6. Right effort.
7. Right mindfulness.
8. Right concentration.

The Right Action forms a list of five fundamental ethical behaviors for all practicing Buddhists to follow. They are:
1. To refrain from destroying living beings.
2. To refrain from stealing.
3. To refrain from sexual misconduct (adultery, rape, etc.).
4. To refrain from false speech (lying).
5. To refrain from intoxicants which lead to heedlessness. (Fundamental Buddhism 1997)

The response to the question, "How do we know what is right and what is wrong?" can be found in the Noble Eightfold Path and the five fundamental ethical behaviors. They guide a Buddhist to pursue an ascetic lifestyle and spiritual perfection. Similar to Hinduism, volunteer program administrators and organizational leadership teams need to structure reward systems that contribute to the fulfillment of a Buddhist's spiritual needs as well as material needs.

CONFUCIANISM WORLDVIEW

Confucianism was founded in the fifth century B.C. by K'ung-Fu-tzu, more commonly known as Confucius. For more than 2000 years, Confucianism was the official ethical system of China. Since the 1949 Communist revolution, the observance of Confucianism has diminished. However, there are still more than 200 million people in China, Korea and Japan that follow the teachings of Confucius. Although it is not a religion, Confucian ideology is deeply embedded in the culture of these countries. The need for high moral and ethical conduct and loyalty to others is the cornerstone of Confucianism. The response to the question, "How do we know what is right and what is wrong?" is rooted in their strong sense of values and ethics regarding loyalty, reciprocal obligations, and honesty in dealing with others.

In Confucian ideology, loyalty and the concept of reciprocal obligations teach that loyalty to one's superiors is rewarded by the superior bestowing "blessings" upon the subordinate. For example, in Japan this ethic is expressed in lifetime employment for loyal employees. Business relationships are networks of interpersonal business contacts that are supported by reciprocal obligations. For example, the close ties between Japanese automobile companies and their component parts suppliers are facilitated by their loyalty and reciprocity agreements which permit them to work together on the entire process of the design, production and distribution of a quality automobile.

The third ethic, honesty, emphasizes that although dishonest behavior may yield short-term benefits, in the long-run dishonesty does not pay and it brings shame upon the dishonest person and his family.

Any person that violates the ethical principles of loyalty, reciprocal obligations and honesty faces social sanctions that tarnish their reputation and prohibit them from drawing on the resources of the network in the future. Relationship-based networks can be helpful in enforcing agreements between businesses and can be even more effective than the legal system. They are very powerful. Thus, organizations or institutions that seek to do business with Chinese, Japanese or Korean entities or want to obtain grants, scholarships, or other forms of financial backing from them should adhere to the Confucian ethical code. It establishes the guidelines for relationships with others.

MORAL JUDGMENTS

Moral judgments about what is right and what is wrong are often the underlying cause of dissensions. This can be evidenced in businesses and organizations by how the workers respond to certain company policies. Such as, those concerned with providing benefits to domestic partners; or offering employment to people that have been in prison; or offering employee assistance for the use of illegal drugs, or the treatment for alcoholism.

When handling issues involving personal beliefs, deciding what is right and what is wrong, it is best to focus on company policy and reach an agreement for compliance. At times, a review of the company's policy will lead to the need to make significant changes. For example, a company policy that pertains to attire, headdresses, hairstyles, beards, tattoos, and other areas of personal appearance should be reviewed to determine if there is a legitimate business reason for the rule. In the absence of a company policy, the issue should be resolved by using the "reasonable person" standard based upon the prevailing culture and worldview. (i.e. What would a reasonable person do?)

SUMMARY

Cultural influences within an organization are multi-dimensional and often difficult to discern. At times, these influences can result in perpetrating micro-iniquities (subtle snubs against someone from another culture based on undetected biases caused by stereotyping and unfair generalizations). As society continues to change and organizations and institutions continue to become more diverse, understanding in the areas of culture, diversity and worldviews will become increasingly more critical to meet the needs and expectations of local communities.

This chapter has provided a general overview of the guiding principles and ideology of the five most influential religions in the world. Also included in the discussion was the philosophy of Confucianism. We highlighted commonalities in these six major worldviews and discussed their ethical systems. Knowledge of the concepts presented here, when utilized effectively, can help to foster cooperative, and trusting relationships with others.

BRIDGE THE PERSONALITY AND GENERATION GAP

T oday's workforce is unique because there are four separate, distinct generations that interact on a daily basis in the execution of their responsibilities. The 21st century generation gap is different from the past where the previous generation grew up to be like their parents. Instead, it is a convergence of four generations that are distinctly different from the others and they each have different views on work/life balance.

Corporations and organizations benefit greatly from having a spectrum of employees that span generational lines. However, this melting pot of multi-generational diversity impacts group dynamics and affects the contributions and work product of a volunteer team, committee, or ad hoc group and the staff members. The ability to blend the generations and unleash their creative potential and at the same time build a collaborative working environment is the challenge that many volunteer program administrators and volunteer managers face, and failure to do so can be a source of conflict among workers. The goals of this chapter are to:

- Present a synopsis on personality types
- Provide an overview of the four generations in the 21st century workforce
- Outline a prescriptive approach to leverage generational differences

I See You

In the Twentieth Century Fox science fiction movie *Avatar,* the theme song is titled *"I See You."* The phrase "I see you" is a reference to a greeting repeatedly used by the Na'vi (the inhabitants of the planet Pandora) in the film. As Jake (one of the characters in the movie) learns to speak Na'vi, he is told that while the phrase literally means "I see you", it is being used figuratively to mean "I see *into* you", and essentially "I understand you". Just as Jake had to learn to see beyond the physical characteristics of the inhabitants of Pandora, it is important to learn to "see into" the multigenerational workforce and to understand their temperament, character, values and beliefs in order to leverage their differences to achieve shared goals.

Seeing others as different from ourselves oftentimes triggers negative attitudes in response to their different temperaments and the way they behave. There are several theories and approaches that have been designed to identify personality traits for the purpose of improving communications. Three of the most popular and practical workforce methods to "see into" and "understand" a person are the *Myers-Briggs Type Indicator®*, *DiSC® Classic* and *Gallup's StrengthsFinder Profile* personality assessments.

Trait theories indicate that people who differ in personality traits may also differ in their approach to conflict and these attributes may impact their behavior during a conflict. It is therefore valuable to be aware of personality-driven behavior tendencies so that one can control and modify them as appropriate in any given situation. The following synopsis of personality types and traits may be useful to understand the kinds of behaviors to expect from different types of personalities.

PSYCHOLOGICAL TYPES

In 1920, a Swiss physician named Carl Jung published *Psychological Types* in which he wrote that people have a multitude of instincts that drive them from within, that causes them to exhibit either "extraversion" or "introversion" behavior. He identified "four basic psychological functions" and classified them as "thinking," "feeling," "sensation," and "intuition." In the early 1950's, Isabel Myers and her mother Kathryn Briggs used Jung's research to develop a questionnaire to identify the traits of different kinds of personality types. They called it the "Myers-Briggs Type Indicator." (Myers 1998)

Myers-Briggs Type Indicator (MBTI)

The Myers-Briggs Type Indicator starts with an assumption that some individuals preoccupy themselves from birth with looking outward at the world, including people, around them (extraversion); while others come into the world paying more attention to what they are thinking and feeling inside (introversion). The Myers-Briggs questionnaire is a behavior analysis assessment that seeks to describe the intellectual and attitudinal approach of the respondents to their environment and the method they use most often (extroversion or introversion) to process information. The level of scores derived from the test indicates how strongly a person prefers one approach over another. Myers defined eight letters and traits as elements of one's personality that are independent of one another. The eight elements are:

E = Extroverted / Expressive   I = Introverted / Reserved
S = Sensory / Observant   N = Intuitive / Introspective
T = Thinking / Tough-minded   F = Feeling / Friendly
J = Judging / Scheduling   P = Perceiving / Probing

In *Please Understand Me II* (Keirsey 1998, 11, 12) the author expands on Myers' research and provides detailed descriptions of each of the sixteen combinations of types of personality which are portrayed in the "Keirsey Four-Types Sorter" as follows:

Four SPs [Artisans]:
ESTP [Promoter], ISTP [Crafter], ESFP [Performer], and ISFP [Composer]
Four SJs [Guardians]:
ESTJ [Supervisor], ISTJ [Inspector], ESFJ [Provider], and ISFJ [Protector]
Four NFs [Idealists]
ENFJ [Teacher], INFJ [Counselor], ENFP [Champion], and, INFP [Healer]
Four NTs [Rationals]

ENTJ [Field Marshal], INTJ [Mastermind], ENTP [Inventor], and INTP [Architect]

Thus, the Myers-Briggs Type Indicator / Keirsey Four-Types Sorter both address thinking and behavior responses based on acquired habits of viewing and responding to the world in general with a belief that certain habits are predominate. The assumption is that a person's actions will instinctively default to their primary personality type regardless of the situation. However, it is also assumed that as these people mature they can learn to use more of the neglected approaches in an effort to increase their capacity to be successful in a variety of situations. This tool offers a process to increase interpersonal effectiveness and individual problem-solving ability by understanding one's self.

DiSC CLASSIC

DiSC® Classic (Inscape 1996) describes how respondents tend to behave when they respond emotionally to their environment, especially when the emotions have to do with how they see themselves in relation to the environment. The level of the score indicates how intensely they react to the perceived relationship. DiSC Dimensions of Behavior provide a nonjudgmental language for exploring behavioral issues across four primary dimensions:

- **Dominance:** Direct and Decisive. D's are strong-willed, strong-minded people who like accepting challenges, taking action, and getting immediate results.
- **Influence:** Optimistic and Outgoing. I's are "people people" who like participating on teams, sharing ideas, and energizing and entertaining others.
- **Steadiness:** Sympathetic and Cooperative. S's are helpful people who like working behind the scenes, performing in consistent and predictable ways, and being good listeners.
- **Conscientiousness:** Concerned and Correct. C's are sticklers for quality and like planning ahead, employing

systematic approaches, and checking and re-checking for accuracy.

The goals of the DiSC assessment are to help team members: (Inscape 1996)

- understand their own behavior
- learn how and when to adapt their behavior
- improve communication
- promote appreciation of differences
- enhance individual and team performance
- reduce conflict

The DiSC Profile graphically depicts each team member's behavioral style and correlates it as to how it affects the others. Once equipped with this knowledge, a person can adapt their behavior to create positive outcomes during their interactions with other team member's behavioral styles. Similar to Gallup's Strengths Finder Profile, this tool can help team members develop and sustain a positive attitude about their work environment and maximize their strengths to maintain harmony.

GALLUP'S STRENGTHS FINDER PROFILE

In the book, *Now Discover Your Strengths,* (Buckingham 2001), the authors created a program to help people identify their talents, build them into strengths and maximize their most dominant personality traits. "Talent is often described as 'a special natural ability or aptitude,' but for the purposes of strength building, we suggest a more precise and comprehensive definition . . . Talent is any recurring pattern of thought, feeling, or behavior that can be productively applied." Thus if a person is instinctively inquisitive, or competitive, or charming, or persistent, or responsible, that is a talent. (Buckingham 2001, 48)

If a person applies a recurring pattern of thought, feeling, or behavior productively and combines it with knowledge and skills, then this natural talent can be turned into a strength. For example, being charming can be productively applied to fund-raising, or to running for a political office, or to managing upward in an organization. If a person knows his strengths, he can invest in training to obtain the knowledge and skills needed to productively utilize his natural talents (similar to a baseball pitcher that hires a coach to perfect his fastball).

The Strengths Finder Profile is similar to both Myers-Briggs Type Indicator and DiSC Profile in that it helps people assess how important it is to understand one's own behavior and how it relates to others. The Strengths Finder Profile is unique because it encourages people to focus on their strengths rather than on their weaknesses. They are able to do this consistently even under stress, and they can do so with ease.

People will commonly focus on their own weaknesses in an attempt to minimize their negative impact, but it is less common for people to focus on their strengths. When they choose to build upon the positive traits they can then achieve even greater success.

The Strengths Finder Profile includes 34 dominant "themes" that systematically reveal sources of satisfaction to a person. Once a person understands his top-five dominant themes then those strengths can be translated into powerful tools to build their own self-confidence. The authors ask the question, "How can you identify your sources of satisfaction?" Then they offer this tip: "When you are performing a particular activity, try to isolate the tense you are thinking in. If all you are thinking about is the present—"When will this be over?"—more than likely you are not using a talent. But if you find yourself thinking in the future, if you find yourself actually anticipating the activity—"When can I do this again?"—it is a pretty good sign that you are enjoying it and that one of your talents is in play." (Buckingham 2001, 75)

It is important for volunteer program administrators and managers to identify the strengths that are needed to accomplish an organization's goals. The Strength Finders Profile is one tool that can be used to properly place individuals on teams in which they can maximize their natural strengths. A person is more likely to find satisfaction as a volunteer in areas where his talents can be utilized. It should be noted however, that training is still a prerequisite. It is still necessary to provide the technical knowledge and soft skills that are needed to successfully accomplish the task and to help people develop new skills.

GENERATIONAL IMPRINTS

Each generation has different strengths and weaknesses. These are derived from the generational imprint that was influenced by major life events and experiences that impacted each new generation. For example:

- Traditionalists/Pre-Baby Boomers (born before 1943) - life experiences were formed by the Great Depression and World War II;
- Baby Boomers (born roughly between 1944-1964) "Me" generation- were influenced by economic prosperity, the assassinations of President Kennedy, Martin Luther King and Bobby Kennedy, and the Viet Nam War;
- Generation X (born roughly between 1965-1981) original "latchkey" generation - attitudes were formed by instability of society's institutions such as marriage and divorce, corporate downsizing, parent's loss of social contract for lifetime employment with one employer, and the crash of the Space Shuttle Challenger;
- Generation Y (born roughly between 1982-2000) - key life experiences revolve around the 9/11 terrorist attacks, changes in homeland security, cutting edge computer technology, and a world where everyone is always connected through the internet, cell phones, social media sites and other modes of technology.

Just as external environmental forces have influenced each consecutive generation; it has also impacted the workplace. Work cultures and work attitudes have evolved over time. This is evidenced by the shift in work/life expectations during the time span of the 4 generations in the 21st Century workplace. The work credo for Pre-Baby Boomer's is "I am my work;" for Baby-

Boomers it's "I live to work;" for Generation X it's "I work to live;" and, for Generation Y it's "I work to play." This shift in workers' mindsets has caused organizational cultures to evolve from being rigid authoritarian entities to becoming flexible work/balance entities. Each generation responds to different motivations based upon its work/life view.

Every generation has a place in the workplace. They are all able to do the job but they may approach the assignment in different ways. Each generation has their own style of work and though different, all styles are proven to be effective. So what does this mean when generations come together in the workplace? Where do they fit in? Can they fit together?

3 STEPS TO SUCCESSFULLY BLEND GENERATIONS

A common problem for volunteer program administrators and managers is to learn how to create an environment where multiple generations understand and adapt to one another's work ethics. A unified, harmonious workforce is beneficial to everyone. There are three essential steps to successfully blending generations: (1) transfer knowledge; (2) understand each generation's core values; and, (3) tailor efforts to increase effectiveness.

Knowledge Transfer:

Oftentimes, older generations retire without transferring their knowledge to the younger generation and yet they are the ones that are responsible for taking their place. As a leader, it is important to instill within volunteers and employees the importance of sharing information and learning from one another. Encourage the younger generation to listen to and learn from the older generation. Establish procedures for the older generation to document their knowledge and ask them to include any helpful tidbits that they have learned throughout their tenure with the company that will facilitate getting the job done without reinventing the wheel.

- **Provide forums to share ideas:** Establish a positive line of communication amongst generations to help to break down the age barrier between the groups.
- **Maximize one another's strengths:** Each generation brings their own strengths to the table. Exhibit a willingness to learn and embrace the strengths of others. Each generation can build off the other's strengths to enlarge the pool of talents.

Understand Generational Core Values

Following is a brief synopsis of each generation's core values:
- **Pre-Baby Boomers:** Dedication and sacrifice, hard work, company loyalty, strong sense of ethics, conservative, respect for authority, delayed gratification, personal reputation.
- **Baby Boomers:** Diligence, education and learning, stable work environment, company loyalty, embrace leadership in terms of hierarchy, community involvement, strong sense of purpose, personal gratification, opportunities for promotion, public recognition, expects tangible rewards for work ethic and long hours.
- **Generation X:** Fierce independence, skepticism, self-motivated, self-sufficient, puts emphasis on self-satisfaction/hard work to make something of themselves, work/life balance, expects individual development, cutting edge technology, wants to realistically make a difference.
- **Generation Y:** Optimistic, confident, educated, articulate, technically literate, flexible working arrangements, equality culture ("everyone is important here"), comfortable within global setting, moral, civic-minded, creative, wants to be part of something meaningful, seeks relevancy.

Tailor Efforts to Increase Effectiveness

Teamwork skills vary enormously from individual to individual. A person may possess the functional skills and the knowledge necessary to fill a position but need guidance on how to be a team player within a given work environment. Thus the selection process is a very important factor in the effort to build cohesive teams. The process that is needed to recruit, train and retrain differs for each generation. Although adherence to the following guidelines cannot guarantee success, it can provide a resource to effectively recruit, train, retrain and manage four different generations of employees and volunteers in the workforce.

Pre-Baby Boomers:

Recruiting and Retaining	Training
• Offer flexible working arrangements • Tell them they are wanted for their age and experience • Go overboard with respect • Use traditional communications • Tap into service orientation	• Will respond to respected leaders • Coach and demonstrate how to use new products, technology • Acknowledge their background and experience • Be patient

Baby Boomers:

Recruiting and Retaining	Training
• Offer flexible working arrangements • Tell them you are looking for someone who can make a difference • Tap into their desire to help change the world • Visible, public recognition and perks are important and valued	• Don't focus on blame – they will tune out • Coach and demonstrate how to use new products, technology • Focus training directly to individual performance and success • Be patient • Teach with equality ("We can

• Use traditional communications	make a difference by…")

Generation X:

Recruiting and Retaining	Training
• Offer flexible working arrangements – tell them "we want you to have a life" • Wants a place to learn, to be creative, to have fun • Training is key – they value training • Do not micro-manage • Use and provide latest technology to communicate and perform the work • Empower them to work offsite	• Nurture and promote self learning • Avoid micro-management training • Provide online web-based training • Use social media tools, videos • Classroom without walls

Generation Y:

Recruiting and Retaining	Training
• Offer flexible working arrangements • Provide leading edge technology • Offer opportunity to be a part of something meaningful • Focus on working collaboratively • Awards are expected • Equality culture ("everyone here is important") • Tap into service orientation	• Incorporate interaction with colleagues • Establish mentor programs • Train with technology • Emphasize "you are special and unique" in training materials • Show relevancy (for training and for the work to be performed)

RISKS OF MISMANAGED MULTI-GENERATIONS IN THE WORKPLACE

Dissension can arise in the workplace if the integration of generations is not properly managed. Conflict can have an overwhelming affect on productivity. For example, Baby Boomers are willing to work long hours and value others who share their beliefs. In contrast, Generation X values work/life balance. As a result of these conflicting beliefs a Baby Boomer may view a Generation X person as someone that lacks commitment or the willingness to do what it takes to get the job done. The tension that may result from these different views could prevent the Baby Boomer from acknowledging the complementary strengths the Generation X employee adds to the team. For example, the Generation X employee's technical aptitude may enable him or her to quickly and efficiently process transactions to achieve time-sensitive performance goals in less time, thereby enabling the team to complete the assignment without having to work long hours.

To keep multiple generations engaged and working together in a productive manner, it is important to embrace their differences. Older generations can be utilized to mentor and support younger, less experienced generations. Due to their years of experience, older generations are capable of foreseeing and diagnosing issues before they become problems or crisis situations.

Misunderstandings and strife can and will occur between members of different generational groups because of varied perspectives. Actions that can be taken to mitigate dissension are:

- See and appreciate the talents, strengths and perspectives of others.
- Create an "equality" (everyone is important) work culture.
- Share wisdom and knowledge generously.
- Lead based on performance not generation grouping.
- Start talking—ask "How do you see me?", "What do you think?"
- Value differences.

As a manager, it is important to keep the lines of communication open so that different opinions can be expressed. An exchange of opinions allows the older generation to bridge the gap between the other generations by combining new ideas with institutional wisdom.

In conclusion, companies that embrace generational differences and include individual development, mentoring, and coaching to meet the needs and interests of each generation are more likely to be able to recruit and retain the best available workers and volunteers.

SECTION 3 – COOPERATIVE RELATIONSHIPS-VOLUNTEERS WANTED

VOLUNTEER PROGRAM ADMINISTRATION

Non-profit organizations rank fourth behind government, business, and labor in terms of people employed. Most non-profit organizations count on the assistance of volunteers to augment their staff to accomplish their work. With the increase in public debt, the decrease in government funds, and the limited amount of donors that are available to meet the growing need to provide resources, volunteers have become a mainstay to fill in the gap and provide these valuable services. The areas in which volunteer support is best utilized are: health, housing, education, youth development, arts and historic works preservation, parks, recreation, environment conservation, religious, and other social services and membership organizations.

Many non-profit and membership organizations have a board of directors that is responsible for organizational policy and they have to authorize expenditures to finance the volunteer program development and staffing. In some organizations all volunteers are managed or supervised by a volunteer coordinator or volunteer program administrator. While in others this function has been decentralized and the coordinator or administrator only supervises the volunteers in the volunteer services department who in turn supervise the local volunteers.

The decentralized model is more common in large non-profit and government organizations because these organizations tend to have multiple locations and therefore the supervision of volunteers is handled at the local level, by a locally designated person. Regardless of whether the supervision of volunteers is centralized or decentralized, for a volunteer program to be successful, at least one individual (i.e. a volunteer program administrator) should be assigned the responsibility for its management.

The best indicator of the Board of Directors and organizational management's support for a volunteer program is the status ascribed to the volunteer program administrator role. Title, pay, and benefits should be equivalent to that of other managers or directors. The volunteer program administrator should report to a senior-level executive and provide periodic updates on the volunteer program(s) to the Board of Directors. The designation of a mid-level or senior-level management position to oversee volunteer services sends a clear message to the employees, volunteers, and the community that the organization values and understands the significance and importance of the contributions of its volunteers. Thus, finding the right person to manage volunteer services is critical to the overall success of an organization's volunteer programs.

THE VOLUNTEER PROGRAM ADMINISTRATOR

The purpose of the volunteer program administrator (coordinator/director/manager/leader of volunteer services) is to be responsible for the organization and management of volunteer services and all aspects of the involvement of volunteers in an organization.

Key areas of responsibility and specific duties of the volunteer program administrator are:

- Program planning and management.
- Budget projections, monthly / annual reports
- Track volunteer assignments and utilization.
- Recruit, interview, screen, select and place volunteers.
- Recognize volunteer achievements.
- Orientation, training, and the development of materials to support these functions.
- Develop policies, procedures and handbooks, as required.
- Supervise office staff and volunteer leaders/managers/supervisors.
- Write and update job/position descriptions.

- Maintain personal contact with department heads, key people in the community.

Volunteer program administrators must understand the mission, purpose, and the style of operation of the organization. They must be able to work cooperatively with staff members at all levels in the organization in order to facilitate positive relationships between the staff and volunteers. They must be able to communicate organizational goals in terms of practical actions and activities and specifically state the tasks that are to be performed by the staff and the volunteers.

Volunteer program administrators are essential to the successful management and integration of volunteers and paid and unpaid staff members. Volunteers may work "for free" but there are costs to overseeing the volunteer program.

SELECTING THE IDEAL VOLUNTEER PROGRAM LEADER

The profile of a volunteer program administrator includes a person who:

- Has integrity, is trustworthy, and has a strong work ethic;
- Understands the mission and style of operation of the organization;
- Is able to translate organizational goals into practical tasks and assignments;
- Has proven leadership and conflict resolution skills;
- Is cordial, courteous, and respectful and has a positive attitude;
- Has strong interpersonal communication and negotiation skills;
- Has good oral and written communication skills;
- Is able to motivate others;
- Takes initiative;
- Is sensitive to others and values diversity;
- Has a sense of humor;

- Handles stress and has good coping skills;
- Shares the organization's values and beliefs; and
- Supports the organization's mission, goals and philosophy.

Finding the right person to manage volunteer services requires the same care and attention as hiring any other professional, key organizational staff member. Once the position has received board approval (if needed) and the job description has been written, then the organization should advertise the position internally and externally (with community agencies, internet job centers, such as VolunteerMatch.com, Monster.com, Yahoo Jobs, etc., and social media networking cites, such as, LinkedIn).

While preference may be given to internal candidates, it may be best to concurrently post the position externally to save time in the event that there are no internal candidates that are qualified to fill the position. This is likely to be true if the person filling the position is required to possess a certificate or certification in volunteer management. The Certified in Volunteer Administration (CVA) credential is available through the Council for Certification in Volunteer Administration (CCVA). For more information see www.cvacert.org. Additional options for advertising the position include the local community college or in regional newspapers for at least one day on a weekend.

Key members of the organizational leadership team should be selected to review the resumes and develop a "short list" (no more than seven) of candidates to interview. The interview panel should include the person that will supervise the volunteer program administrator and at least one department head, one staff member, and one experienced volunteer. Panel members should each have a copy of the applicant's resume and they should meet in advance to agree upon the list of questions that each applicant will be asked to answer (the same core questions should be asked of each applicant). In addition to the basic "Tell us about yourself, your skills, your experience" type of questions, the person being interviewed should be asked situational questions to give the panel an opportunity to assess how the person responds to "real life" scenarios. At the conclusion of all of the interviews, the interview panel should make their selection and once an offer has been made and accepted, all the other candidates should be notified and thanked for their interest in the position.

ORIENTATION AND ONBOARDING PROCESS

The orientation and onboarding process for the volunteer program administrator should include a review of the organization's mission, vision, goals, hierarchy, chain-of-command protocols, key contacts, and an overview of the full operation of the organization. It is important that the volunteer program administrator understands the organization's values, beliefs and client-service philosophy.

An important part of the onboarding process is for the volunteer program administrator to meet with staff members and keep them informed about the volunteer program developments throughout the process. The staff may express concerns about volunteer recruitment, placement, screening, supervision, confidentiality agreements, orientation, training, or other things specific to their department. They may also have fears about being replaced by volunteers. It will be necessary to calm fears and obtain the commitment from the staff to support the volunteer programs. One way to do this is to involve the staff in defining volunteer tasks and responsibilities and to be willing to let them identify jobs that are appropriate for volunteers. The jobs must be meaningful, clearly defined and within the scope of training provided to volunteers.

The development of the volunteer program will require the permanent staff to expand or change the way things are done to accommodate the volunteers. As such, they should be recognized for accepting the new and possibly additional work associated with the inclusion of volunteers in their department. If they can see the benefits (e.g. additional administrative help, more client support) then they are more likely to embrace the volunteer program and encourage others to support it.

ORGANIZATIONAL PHILOSOPHY
REGARDING VOLUNTEERS

The volunteer program administrator should be able to articulate the organization's philosophy on why it chooses to use the services of volunteers. The philosophy will likely be linked to the volunteer position's job description, the roles and responsibilities of the position, and the expectations of the paid staff. A volunteer program administrator must be able to clearly state in a meaningful, positive way the organization's strategy for augmenting its staff with volunteers so that volunteers are valued and seen as the "real staff" and not as "only a volunteer."

A story about the "only a volunteer" syndrome was shared by Tom Konrad, President, Volunteer Council, Calvert Marine Museum, Solomons, MD (Lee and Catagnus 1999, 16). Mr. Konrad shares the following insights:

"In the case of volunteers, this attitude is evident when they hesitate to make suggestions or voice criticism because they are "only volunteers." This indicates a feeling that their suggestions are not worthwhile or won't be taken seriously. It shows that the volunteer considers him or herself as somewhat of a second-class citizen. . .

The "only a volunteer" attitude may show up in the paid staff as well. True, they may have the responsibility for the success of their programs and are the ones held accountable. However, their attitude cannot be "I am staff and you are only a volunteer so don't bother me with your suggestions." This is a sure way to discourage volunteers from feeling that they are an essential part of any organization and, in fact, are partners with the paid staff in making their place of involvement the best it can be. The "only a volunteer" attitude is wrong on the part of both volunteers and staff and has no place anywhere. Let's be sure we never hear that phrase again."

Volunteers need to feel that they are an essential part of the organization. When volunteers know the same level of excellence is expected of them as all other employees, they are more likely to feel as though they are a part of the team so that they will strive to do their best.

An organization's philosophy on volunteers is further expressed in the terms it uses to describe its' volunteers. In *Supervising Volunteers: An Action Guide for Making Your Job Easier* (Lee and Catagnus 1999, 2), the authors discourage saying you "use" or "utilize" volunteers. Tools and things are used, but not people. In their book, the authors provided the following list of acceptable verbs developed by a colleague, Ivan Scheier that can be put into practice by those that supervise volunteers and the paid staff:

empower	allow
count on	involve
rely on	authorize
ask	mobilize
commission	assign
enable	enlist
delegate to	request
entrust	encourage

The above list of terms may be useful to shift the mindset of staff members from the view that volunteers are "only a volunteer" or "free help" and see them as appreciated, respected, valuable team members.

VOLUNTEERISM DEFINED

Volunteerism is a form of philanthropy or support that involves time, talent and commitment. It has a measurable dollar value in terms of service performed. Volunteers contribute substantially to the gross national product via services rendered and work produced. While volunteers do not receive a salary, there is a cost associated with recruitment, selection, pre-employment screening (such as background checks), training, evaluation, supervision, retention, and recognition of volunteers.

Not all people who work without pay consider themselves volunteers. For example, managing a school board or serving on the board of directors for a non-profit organization is often an unpaid position. Although most people that fill these positions do so to benefit the community or the entity they serve, they also have an obligation or duty to fulfill the duties of the position. They are volunteers in the legal sense of the word with regard to not receiving monetary compensation, other than reimbursement for expenses or a small stipend, yet they are bound by their personal oath to fulfill the term of their commitment. A legal definition of a volunteer is "a participant in something who is not legally bound to participate and does not expect to be paid."

A volunteer generally offers a service of his or her own free will without compulsion. However, there are some volunteers that are motivated to sign up by a court referral, a school graduation requirement or a welfare-to-work program. Some people volunteer at school or church to receive some other form of credit for their volunteer time. Volunteering encompasses various terms such as helper, aide, intern, auxiliary worker, docent, tutor, mentor, or activist, just to name a few. There are numerous volunteer activities and entities that rely upon the services of a volunteer staff to augment the work of the paid staff. Whatever the motivation, volunteers are the "people power" of an organization and are essential to its execution of day-to-day activities. The role of the volunteer program administrator is crucial to ensure volunteers are engaged, motivated, and productive, valuable members of the team.

BENEFITS DERIVED FROM VOLUNTEERS

Volunteers will be attracted to and stay with an organization that takes seriously their desire and ability to do a good job. They want work that is both challenging and stimulating. If there is insufficient work available for the volunteer, then the volunteer should be notified in advance and given an opportunity to take the day off. If the volunteer does not find the work to be personally satisfying, the volunteer will feel his or her time is being wasted and will seek another volunteer position.

Volunteers are vital because they can fill special needs and allow an organization to extend its budget to accomplish tasks which are important to individual clients, tasks that might otherwise go undone. Some typical activities of volunteers in various organizations include:

- Religious – responsible for nursery, child care, summer camps, teaching, food banks, food and clothing distribution, music, administrative assistance.
- Education and youth development – volunteers organize Royal Rangers, Girl Scouts, Boy Scouts, etc. activities, serve on college and university boards, help with after school programs, school trips, and tutoring programs.
- Health and wellness – work in hospitals, nursing homes, senior citizen community centers, provide support for major health-related organizations concerned with diseases such as cancer, heart disease, muscular disorders, etc.
- Employment – serve as mentors, coaches, provide training, employment counseling.
- Arts, culture, humanities – assist in museums, galleries, libraries, theaters, community television and radio stations, art and literary councils, historical preservation societies.
- Environment, wildlife, park preservation – assist at animal shelters to provide animal care and protection, involved in conservation of resources and recycling, maintain parks, plant trees, assist with forestry services.
- Law and justice – provide victim support, provide legal services and crime prevention education, provide chaplain and other ministry services in prisons.
- Membership Organizations – provide a wide array of services for practitioners and consultants in numerous

professions, such as human resources, accounting, hospitality, and trade organizations, such as unions.

Although the above list is not all-inclusive, it sheds light on the span of organizations and institutions that rely upon volunteer services. Effective volunteer management is essential to the continued operation of many of these entities.

Volunteer relationships are successful when volunteers are in jobs they want to do, and when they look forward to working with the others that are involved. Volunteers should always be shown appreciation for their work. Thank them for their work and let them know that the place would not be the same without them. Lack of funds should not be the reason to add volunteers to the staff because then they will be viewed as temporary workers that are only in place until the "real" staff is hired. Such a philosophy demoralizes both the paid staff and the volunteers because they are not viewed as being the organization's first choice. Since most organizations have limited resources, it may be important to spend a moment to focus on a few of the benefits derived from relying on volunteers. Volunteers offer:

- A wide-range of backgrounds and diversity, in terms of age, race, social background, income, educational level, political influence, and so forth, that enables them to provide a broader, outsider's perspective of the work and services provided by the organization.
- The ability to increase the amount of service offered in terms of extended hours or days of operation.
- Skills or talents that expand those of existing employees, such as webmaster, or social media networking capabilities (while web-based services are necessary in the 21st Century work environment, not all organizations are able to fund them).
- Community outreach and special events support.
- Access, as private citizens, to global communities without the bureaucratic, jurisdictional restrictions that paid employees may have.

- A network of people, business and community contacts.

The wide-range of benefits that can be derived from volunteers can best be fully realized if an organization has a qualified volunteer program administrator that oversees the selection and placement of volunteers. Therefore, it is essential to recruit, screen, and select the appropriate volunteer for each position.

VOLUNTEER JOB DESCRIPTIONS

The job description provides explicit details of the volunteer position. It should be written before the hiring process begins to ensure that the department head has thought out exactly what is expected of the person filling the position, and the volunteer's relationship to the other staff members and the overall organization.

The volunteer's "position description" or "volunteer role expectations" should provide a written explanation of what is required to do a good job. Each volunteer position should have a written job description. The title of the job description should reflect what the volunteer does, e.g., receptionist, guest services assistant, tutor, driver, or nursery aide. The word "volunteer" should not appear in the title.

The vision statement of the organization and the goals of the work unit or team should be stated in the job description. This will help the volunteer to understand the overall scope and purpose of the work that is being performed and it reinforces the connection between the work the volunteer performs with the work or services provided by the rest of the team and the organization.

A statement of why the position exists and what the volunteer is expected to accomplish should be included followed by a list of the specific tasks and activities that the volunteer needs to do to meet the expectations of the position.

The minimum requirements for the position, such as, skills, background, experience, training, minimum hours per week or month, specific hours/days of the week the volunteer must be present, essential job functions, etc. must be included. Also, state if the successful completion of a criminal background check, and drug/alcohol screening are required.

If the position has restrictions that prohibit certain actions, the volunteer needs to be made aware of these restrictions in advance. This may include such things as providing medical information or advice to patients, their families or visitors, or bringing their children with them to work, or any other restriction that is relevant to the job (such as a maximum term-limit to serve or occupy a position). This type of information needs to be included in the position description.

The purpose of the job description is to outline the core roles and responsibilities of the position. This will eliminate confusion with regards to the hours of work and the length of the assignment, and will notify potential applicants of pre-employment screening requirements. Each volunteer should be given a copy of the job description.

Job descriptions should be reviewed periodically to determine if they accurately reflect the work to be performed and the expectations of the management. This is especially true if there is a high turnover rate in a particular position. It is important to ask volunteers if the work is different from what they expected. There may be an opportunity to redesign the job to make it more meaningful and increase volunteer retention.

VOLUNTEER RECRUITMENT AND PLACMENT

The ability to select the right volunteer for the right position is one the greatest challenges for a volunteer program administrator because people often do not understand the volume and scope of the work tied to a specific volunteer position and when their expectations are not met they leave unexpectedly.

One way to minimize misunderstandings over the contributions and valuable assistance provided by the volunteer workforce is to host an "open house" for prospective volunteers.

Those who attend will learn about volunteer positions prior to the filling of those vacancies. At the open house, the volunteer program administrator should discuss the job descriptions, the quality of the training, and the organization's commitment to providing a safe, fun, enjoyable place for its volunteers to work. They should also express their sincere appreciation for the work performed by its volunteers. Part of the agenda should also include an upbeat presentation by seasoned volunteers who can share stories about what they like about the work. They should also speak candidly about the difficult, yet rewarding aspects of the position.

The open house is a forum to discuss in a positive manner the position description and provide the participants with an opportunity to ask questions about the position. At the conclusion of the open house, the participants will have a realistic view of the work that is expected and they can set realistic expectations on what they hope to accomplish by joining the team. The participants should be given an information packet that includes an application form (or information for online applications) and the job descriptions of vacant positions. They should be encouraged to apply if they are still interested.

The benefit of hosting the open house is that the participants that apply for the vacancies will be highly motivated and knowledgeable about the position. Motivated volunteers are more likely to fulfill their commitment and complete their assignments. Unlike permanent employees, the volunteers will often depart once the work is complete. Retention is relative only to each assignment and each volunteer. Thus, it is imperative to do all possible to select the right person for the right position.

VOLUNTEER ORIENTATION

The goals of the orientation session are to make the volunteer feel welcome and to provide them with the information they need to become comfortable in their new environment. Volunteers need to know what is expected of them and how their tasks relate to the organization or the community they serve. During the on-the-job orientation session, the volunteers are provided with a working knowledge of the organization, staff, location and other information relevant to the position.

Volunteer orientation should include:

- an overview of general rules, regulations, policies and procedures
- a tour of the work area, including where the volunteer will sit, work, and store personal items if the position is on-site
- location of supplies, equipment, and tools the volunteer is authorized to use
- the names and responsibilities of co-workers
- the process to check-in and check-out for the work assignment
- policies on smoking, eating, the use of cellphones and personal laptops at work
- the names and titles of any VIPs that the volunteer should be aware of
- the volunteer's supervisor's name and contact information
- a list of "who to call" in case of an emergency or to request assistance and their contact information

The orientation session is designed to minimize time that is wasted trying to find out what is needed to do the job or making errors because of the lack of information. The orientation session should be mandatory for new volunteers prior to beginning their new assignment. It is also a good opportunity to introduce the new volunteers to staff and experienced volunteers (be sure everyone wears a name tag). Volunteers should not have to "learn by accident" or be left to figure things out for themselves. They deserve the courtesy of the time and attention that is necessary to feel welcomed and comfortable in their new environment.

Volunteers new to the organization will also need a review of the evacuation and other safety procedures and a chance to practice using safety equipment, if needed. No matter how short-term the assignment may be, at a minimum, all volunteers should be given a brief on-the-job orientation of basic information, and an explanation of evacuation and safety procedures.

VOLUNTEER TRAINING

The development and delivery of training materials for volunteers is the function of the volunteer program administrator in collaboration with experienced volunteers, staff, supervisors and other key people who understand the demands and goals of the position. The goals of the training should be to increase knowledge, improve skills, and raise the level of competency of the volunteer staff.

The ability to communicate with clarity is required to ensure that the volunteer clearly understands the tasks associated with the job assignment in order to be successful. In *Christian Education Principles & Practice* (DeKoven 1996, 96), the author, Dr. Stan DeKoven, wrote the following regarding "clarity":

"A skilled instructor has the ability to understand when students are confused or unable to follow a certain point, and will with skill and sensitivity eradicate the confusion, thus enlarging their ability to understand. This can be accomplished in a number of ways, including the presentation of alternative explanations or utilizing illustrations that will clarify. Sometimes, it is the ability to take an idea, break it down into smaller bits, and then reintegrate it as a whole picture which makes instruction easier to follow and understand. Truly gifted instructors are able to make things relevant to the student."

Experienced volunteers can offer insight into the gaps they have discovered in their personal knowledge or in the necessary skill requirements for the position and make recommendations on the training the volunteers need to receive. Training in the areas of decision-making, effective oral and written communication techniques, team building, conflict resolution and dealing with stress, anger or trauma are all topics that apply to a wide range of volunteer positions.

The training should be scheduled at a time that is convenient for the volunteers in recognition of the fact that many of them have full-time jobs during the day. At the conclusion of the training, the volunteers should be asked to evaluate the class to determine if the volunteer felt it would be useful in their volunteer assignment. The overarching goals of the training should be to improve the volunteer's confidence and motivation so they feel competent to carry out their assignments and to facilitate personal growth.

VOLUNTEER RECOGNITION

Recognition and rewards are important to volunteers. They appreciate receiving credit for a job well done. Always thank them for their help before they leave. Express sincere gratitude. Be sure to attend recognition ceremonies and designated "volunteer appreciation days" to celebrate their accomplishments. Timely recognition and genuine concern for volunteers will contribute to their longevity of service and make everyone's job easier and more rewarding. Also, positive accolades may inspire others to volunteer in the future.

In *Leading Today's Volunteers: Motivate and Manage Your Team* (MacLeod and Hogarth 1999, 148-151), the authors offer five principles for "rewarding and acknowledging volunteers." They are:

1. Build acknowledgement into volunteer management
2. "Adopt policies that reflect a philosophy of treating volunteers as important partners in the organization. The elements of good management convey an attitude of respect for volunteers, the work they do, the value of their experience, opinion, and outlook."
3. Offer opportunities for growth and challenge,
4. "Volunteers are most likely to feel appreciated when taken seriously. Increasingly, the prime motivation prompting volunteer involvement is the desire to learn. People

respond to increased responsibility, input to decision making, and opportunities to influence the direction of the program and, possible, the organization."

5. Day-to-day acknowledgement,
6. "Recognition involves day-to-day acknowledgement as well as periodic formal gestures of appreciation. Verbal appreciation, sincerely expressed, is a most meaningful form of recognition. It is particularly valuable immediately following any extraordinary effort, accomplishment, or success by a volunteer. . . People appreciate being individually acknowledged, being addressed by name, included in conversations, and generally treated like a member of the organization."
7. Give tangible rewards,
8. "Many volunteers sincerely appreciate traditional ways of saying thank you such as letters of thanks, plaques, certificates, and pins for long service. Other more practical awards which are equally appreciated are business cards, name badges, a parking space, a picture on a photo board, discount in a gift shop, or profile in a newsletter, local newspaper, or other media."
9. Organize recognition events,
10. "The traditional annual volunteer's lunch, dinner, coffee party, or similar event is a mainstay of the volunteer world. Invite families and give awards, gifts, or make other meaningful presentations."

In summary, it is everyone's job to look for ways to celebrate creativity, innovation, accomplishments, courage, loyalty, commitment and long-term service, in a meaningful, sincere manner. Recognition research shows that there are few methods of recognition that are as appreciated as a personal hand-written note about a particular task well-done.

Look for new ideas to express a genuine message of appreciation that truly makes the volunteer feel wanted, needed, and appreciated. Celebrate success!

21ST CENTURY VOLUNTEER LEADERSHIP

Powerful leaders act with integrity and are perceived as honest, reliable and trustworthy. They demonstrate courage and determination. They empower others, encourage creativity and innovation, and foster alliances and business partnerships. They inspire unity and the achievement of a shared vision, and arouse others to strive to attain breakthrough goals.

In *Leaders that Conquer* (Maldonado 2004, 40, 41), the author describes a leader as a person who:

- Encourages with words of affirmation at the precise time when it is most needed
- Influences others through inspiration
- Motivates others through words of faith to do difficult tasks
- Directs by example
- Guides through vision and purpose
- Persuades people to follow the vision
- Has passion and drive to accomplish the vision
- Disciplines and corrects when needed

PURPOSE-CENTERED LEADERSHIP

Purpose-centered leadership motivates others to accomplish the thing they purpose in their hearts to achieve. The benefit of purpose-centered leadership is a fully engaged workforce. In an organization guided by purpose-centered leaders, all employees (paid staff and volunteers) have a clear understanding of the connection between their job, their individual contribution, and the organization's overall strategic mission and vision. Where gaps exist, the purpose-centered leader actively involves the employees (paid staff and volunteers) in identifying the root causes of disengagement and then removes any obstacles that prevent them from effectively contributing to the organization's success.

CRITICAL THINKING SKILLS

Volunteer program administrators must be critical thinkers in order to create an environment of cooperation, commitment, and trust. This is essential for collaboration with community groups, special interest coalitions, informal leaders, and others to achieve the organization's success. They must have the ability to evaluate information, make it relevant, and disseminate it in a manner that positively influences all of the stakeholders.

Following are a few keys to developing critical thinking skills taken from *God's Unfolding Battle Plan,* (Pierce 2007, 53, 54):

1. Define your problem and clarify your real concern.
2. Evaluate all the information you have and then pinpoint the missing pieces so that you can develop a complete thought process.
3. Define your traps and biases.
4. Clarify your position and authority.
5. Identify the root causes of the problem you are addressing.
6. Determine what point of view you are using in your analysis.
7. Be willing to shift your perspective at any time.
8. Ask yourself, *Am I limiting my thought processes to only what I know?* Limited thought processes are synonymous with self-righteousness.
9. Identify anything that you are taking for granted in your analysis. Do not allow your assumptions to cause you to be foolish.
10. Check to make sure that you are not making intellectual judgments based on partial truths.
11. Ask yourself, *Have I simplified things to the point that I'm missing out on the major component here?*
12. Avoid being biased or prejudiced in the way you receive, perceive and release information.

Actions reflect a person's thinking. Therefore, it is important to possess critical thinking skills to discern who or what is attempting to influence a person's thoughts; and, thus their actions.

Critical thinking skills enable the volunteer program administrator to effectively assess and advocate change and resolve differences. Critical thinking involves "keeping both an open mind to new revelation and adhering to the established safeguards of the mind that have been constructed throughout years of living. . . Richard Paul and Linda Elder, who are authors and internationally renowned experts in the field of critical thinking, offer a comprehensive description of a critical thinker," that states: (Pierce 2007, 48)

"A well-cultivated critical thinker raises vital questions and problems, gathers and assesses relevant information, and can effectively interpret it; comes to well-reasoned conclusions and solutions, testing them against relevant criteria and standards; thinks open-mindedly within alternative systems of thought, recognizing and assessing as need be, their assumptions, implications and practical consequences; and communicates effectively with others in figuring out solutions to complex problems."

The heart of critical thinking is the process of asking questions that challenge assumptions and to carefully consider the responses. Critical thinking is one of the most important skills that an effective purpose-centered leader can possess.

PROJECT MANAGEMENT

Many of the functions of volunteers are project driven. A practical application of critical thinking can be demonstrated by looking at the process of project management. Every project has a life cycle. Six key steps in the project planning process are:
1. Project definition – define the output
2. Task identification – define the work
3. Task elimination – define the resources

4. Project scheduling – define the timeline / milestones on a calendar
5. Contingency planning – examine the risks
6. Project trade-off – optimize the plan

Each step of the project planning process requires asking questions, examining alternative solutions, and conducting a cost/benefit analysis before reaching agreement on the optimal outcome. The benefit of using a project management process to identify the elements of the work for the project is that it gives the stakeholders and volunteer program administrator an opportunity to strategically assess the tactical aspects of each assignment and define the roles and responsibilities of everyone that will be involved in the implementation and delivery of the service.

Another benefit of mapping out tasks is that it highlights redundancies and areas where work overlaps. It also provides a renewed understanding of the business' performance and identifies functions that need to be redesigned to better align with the organization's vision and goals. Finally, it is a useful tool that can be used to identify areas that have performance, retention, and attrition issues as they relate to job design. The outcome of the project management process should be to establish a high-performance relationship among the organizational leadership team, the paid staff and volunteers, and the organization's stakeholders.

LEADERSHIP RESPONSIBILITIES

There is a magnetism involved in volunteering that draws people to certain volunteer opportunities. A purpose-centered leader will tap into that energy and help the volunteers reach their potential and help them feel rewarded and valued for their involvement. As discussed in the previous chapter, the volunteer program administrator (coordinator/manager) is responsible for the volunteer program and is the primary liaison between the paid staff and volunteers.

Key leadership responsibilities for a volunteer program administrator include setting the direction, focusing on the commitment to the organizational vision, communicating and interpreting the vision so that others will align with it, and training for excellence. They create an engaged network of people and relationships to accomplish the vision. As the key link between the organization's leadership team and its volunteers, the volunteer program administrator has the responsibility to be an advocate to the volunteer. This includes efforts within the organization and to remove obstacles so that the client's needs are met, the volunteer's aspirations are achieved, and the organization's vision is realized.

SETTING AND COMMUNICATING EXPECTATIONS

Volunteers—like all workers—need to know what is expected of them and they need to be empowered to do the job so they can feel pride in what they have accomplished. The job description should describe the responsibilities of the position, the system of supervision and accountability, and the means to measure performance. It should also clarify how each position contributes to the attainment of organizational goals eliminating confusion over role expectation of both the volunteers and paid staff.

In *Leadership and Management of Volunteer Programs* (Fisher and Cole 1993, 34, 35), the authors cite four key elements for the effective design of positions for volunteers:

1. Provide the volunteer with a sense of "turf."
2. Ensure the volunteer has the opportunity and authority to think about as well as perform the job. Thinking includes planning, organizing, deciding, and evaluating.
3. Assure the position description communicates responsibility to achieve results linked directly to the agency's mission and goals, rather than simply to perform a list of activities.
4. Provide a clear understanding of how to measure the success of an effort and one's participation in it so the

volunteer will be able to assess the value of his or her own contribution.

Volunteers are generally self-motivated and appreciate clear direction and freedom to accomplish their assignments. They are more likely to lose interest in the job if they are micro-managed. They value having an accessible and approachable leader that is available when needed but who gives them the freedom to make decisions. However, they need to understand that there is a balance between freedom and authority. This freedom must be balanced by the amount of the authority and structure that is necessary to effectively and efficiently complete the assignment.

BUILDING HIGH PERFORMANCE TEAMS

Highly engaged employees strive for great results. The best way to achieve an amicable long-term working relationship is to reach a mutual agreement beforehand to discuss concerns when they first arise rather than to allow them to go unaddressed. Having an established process in place allows people to voice their grievances and differences and fosters a respectful, cooperative work environment. It provides valuable feedback to the organizational leadership team (including the volunteer program administrator) on problems before they have the opportunity to escalate into conflicts.

It is important that the organizational leadership team constructively manages conflict by promptly addressing actions that cause strife and discontent in the workplace. Conflict avoidance never resolves the problem. The manner in which leaders respond to willful acts that create conflict is crucial. If this conduct goes unchecked, it will undermine trust.

Trust can be broken when people sense their leader is smoothing over or condoning someone else's willful and intentional inappropriate behavior. A passive leader is not a leader. Effective leaders, whether they are volunteer leaders, hospital administrators, pastors, school principals, deans, or CEOs hold people accountable for their actions. They are responsible for assessing both paid staff member and volunteers' relationships with one another and with external constituents.

When expectations are not being met private counseling sessions should be held to provide objective feedback and to clarify roles, responsibilities and expectations. Establishing specific and realistic goals outlining a process for achievement minimizes opportunities for conflict. The goal of any coaching session should be to help the person become a top-performer. Both the organization's reputation and the person's reputation are at stake. Therefore, it is important to identify the issues that are causing the discontent and correct them.

CONSTRUCTIVE CONFRONTATIONS

In the book, *Conflict Management: A Communication Skills Approach* (Borisoff and Victor 1989) the authors propose a model for conflict management that consists of the following five steps:
1. Assessment
2. Acknowledgment
3. Attitude
4. Action
5. Analysis

Using their model, we will discuss the actions that could be taken in response to a volunteer's unsatisfactory performance. In the assessment phase, the volunteer program administrator has to decide whether a volunteer's disagreeable behavior should be acknowledged or ignored. Phase 1 is important when dealing with volunteers because if the volunteer program administrator incorrectly assesses the behavior and confronts the volunteer, then the relationship may be permanently damaged. It is important to base the assessment on the facts related to the specific incident.

In the next phase, the volunteer program administrator acknowledges the volunteer's behavior that needs to be addressed. Next, the volunteer program administrator demonstrates a willingness to discuss the disagreement and to hear the volunteer's perspective without bias. During the discussion, the volunteer program administrator observes the volunteer's actions, such as non-verbal cues, in an effort to determine if the person agrees or disagrees with what is being said. The purpose of the discussion is to have an open two-way dialogue about the issue and to discuss various actions that can be taken to remedy the situation. And finally, the volunteer program administrator analyzes all of the concerns expressed and summarizes and clarifies the agreement that has been reached to manage the conflict.

Constructive confrontations should be held in a private location. Prior to the meeting, the person conducting the meeting should gather solid information that has been validated. This is necessary to ensure that the facts are not being misrepresented. The conversation should be kept on track and focused on the solution to the problem. It is crucial to only attack the problem, not the person. The person conducting the meeting should listen and remain calm, focused and in control at all times. Difficult conversations will occur in all organizations. However, when a person cares enough to confront in a caring manner, then constructive confrontations can take place and success can be achieved.

Relevancy

Relevancy is very important to volunteers. It is the role of the volunteer program administrator to assign meaningful tasks and to be able to clearly explain the actions that are required to perform the work. It may be useful to seek feedback from the volunteer and to listen to his or her thoughts on the process. The open dialogue not only ensures understanding it also engenders feelings of empowerment and ownership of the results.

The organization's success is the foundation upon which a performance counseling session is based. Some key success factors to share with the volunteer that can help them become more successful are to:

- Understand the organization's culture

- Always be in a mode of learning
- Ask for help
- Be helpful
- Want to make a difference
- Want to make an impact
- Do the right thing – be truthful, honest and a person of integrity

Positive feedback that taps into the organization's mission and the important contributions that the volunteer can make as a part of the organization's success may allow barriers to surface. These barriers may be the root reason of why the volunteer is not providing optimal service.

There are various means to help volunteers remain engaged and become top-performers, such as, to provide developmental training, relevant reference material, mentors, job-shadowing opportunities, feedback, evaluations, and timely informational updates. Each of these options should be discussed with the volunteer to determine what can be done to help them achieve a level of peak performance and commitment.

EMPLOYEE ENGAGEMENT

The Corporate Leadership Council (CLC) completed a global study of the engagement level of 50,000 employees around the world. This study was based on a new, more precise definition of engagement and its direct impact on both employee performance and retention. (CLC 2004, 4)

The Council defines engagement as, "the extent to which employees commit to something or someone in their organization, how hard they work, and how long they stay as a result of that commitment." (CLC 2004, 5) The CLC model of engagement states that "engagement drivers determine rational and emotional commitment which in turn leads to effort and intent to stay resulting in improved performance and retention." (CLC 2004, 5).

One of the key messages taken from the CLC study is, "While employees' commitment to their manager is crucial to engagement, the manager is most important as the enabler of employees' commitment to their jobs, organizations, and teams." (CLC 2004, 4) Although this study was conducted to analyze employee performance and retention, this finding is equally significant for volunteer program administrators or other leaders that manage volunteers because it can also be used to understand the impact that leadership has on the volunteer's commitment to the organization.

The CLC report further states that "emotional engagement is four times more valuable than rational engagement in driving employee effort" (CLC 2004, 4) which can be especially true for volunteers since their passion is often their motivation to serve. The volunteer program administrator can tap into the volunteer's passion and emotional state during recruitment and after the volunteer joins the team. This will inspire employee engagement which in turn will keep the volunteer highly committed to the organization's success.

Some of the characteristics of a highly engaged person are: they demonstrate a willingness to help others with heavy workloads; they volunteer for other duties; and, they look for other ways to do their jobs more effectively.

While commitment to the manager is often pointed out as the key driver of engagement, the Council's research found that the manager plays a more important role as enabler of the emotional commitment of the employee to the job, the team, and the organization. Most important among the 25 highest impact drivers of engagement are: (CLC 2004, 12, 13)

- Connection between work and organizational strategy
- Importance of job to organizational success
- Understanding of how to complete work projects

The CLC study also showed some other factors that were critical in helping increase employee engagement, those factors were: a manager's reputation of honesty and integrity, an organization that has a culture of innovation, internal communications and a strong commitment to diversity.

Employee engagement is essential to an organization's success. To maximize the contributions of the volunteers, the volunteer program administrator should identify the opportunities and the barriers in the current structure; restructure roles to support employee engagement; and, formulize position / job descriptions to tap into the emotional commitment that the volunteers have to the organization's continued success. Equipped with these key findings taken from the CLC report, the volunteer program administrator can be a conduit. They can use this vital information to ensure that what matters most to volunteers is the focus of the volunteer programs, and also to those responsible for their day-to-day job assignments and supervision. The supervisors and volunteer program administrator can create opportunities for the volunteers that will allow them to make meaningful contributions in their work and remain fully engaged.

CONCLUSION

Volunteer management in the 21st Century is both dynamic and rewarding. The purpose of this book is to provide practical guidance on the unique temperament, character and commitment of the four generations of 21st Century volunteers that are in the workplace and how to tap into their desire to make a meaningful difference and achieve the mark of their higher calling.

This book offers relevant, realistic, and useful methods, models and techniques on how to keep volunteers motivated and supportive of the organization's vision and goals. This is in concert with the paid staff. Also presented are the ways to resolve conflicts between the volunteer staff when dissension does occur. It is meant to offer guidance to the organizational leadership teams and volunteer program administrators enabling them to have an actively engaged and totally committed workforce that strives for excellence.

It is my hope, that this book will become an important reference source that will be beneficial to organizational leaders, volunteer managers and volunteer program administrators alike, helping you to understand how to unite and ignite four generations of 21st Century volunteers.

APPENDIX A
Study Guide

Section 1 – Cooperation Begins With Communication

1. Describe the shifts in the methods of communication in the past 30 years. What are the implications of these shifts for non-profit organizations?
2. How have changes in technology contributed to improved communications? How have these changes detracted from improved communications?
3. How might the Internet and the associated World Wide Web and social media networking sites affect global non-profit organizations?
4. Ultimately, understanding individual needs, interests, and goals is at the root of all communications. Evaluate this statement.
5. Most people make decisions on the basis of good reasons, which vary depending on the communication situation, media, and credibility of the source of the communications. Describe the factors that you consider when you assess the credibility of a message. How do your judgmental biases impact your assessment?
6. In general, there are three types of motivation: fear motivation, incentive motivation, and attitude motivation. Describe a situation in which each type of motivation would be appropriate.
7. What roles do ethics play in decision-making?
8. Social psychologist Fritz Heider developed the Attribution Theory. He wrote that people constantly draw inferences about why people do what they do by making personality judgments based upon observed behavior. Discuss your views on the Attribution Theory.
9. Working together collaboratively to create messages that are intended for multiple constituencies can be an effective

strategic communications tool. What are the benefits of joint communications? What are the barriers to joint communications?

10. Write a paragraph on your views concerning the statement, "Cooperation begins with communication."

Section 2 – Working Together in Unity

1. Confrontation is a necessary stimulation to jog one out of mediocrity or to prod one back from extremes. Evaluate this statement.

2. Give an example of how confrontation can be used constructively to reenergize a non-profit organization.

3. In your own words, describe "Interactive Engagement."

4. Assumptions are a set of beliefs shared by a group that causes the group to think and act in certain ways. Make a list of assumptions that you have about a business or organization that you support. How might these assumptions hinder that business or organization from embracing change?

5. The exposure of a long-held assumption that is rooted in the mindset that says "we've always done it this way" is the first step in creating an environment for change. Evaluate this statement.

6. What is the purpose of collaborative problem-solving? Give an example.

7. The five-points for "breakthrough negotiation" are: 1) Don't react; 2) Don't argue; 3) Don't reject; 4) Don't push; and, 5) Don't escalate. Describe how each point can contribute to reaching a mutually agreeable win-win solution to a problem.

8. Emotions impact conflict. What are some inappropriate emotional responses to conflict?

9. Disagreements are a normal part of developing and maintaining a relationship. Give examples of how to win the cooperation of others and positively resolve conflicts.

10. Conflict resolution is a shared responsibility. Everyone has a duty and an active, positive role to play to ensure the success of an organization. Write a paragraph that discusses your views on this statement.
11. Describe why it is important to understand the personal values, beliefs and culture of others to work together in unity.
12. Discuss your views on the "pros and cons" concerning the three theories that were discussed in Chapter 8, that have been designed to identify personality traits for the purpose of improving communications.
13. What impact did the discussion on the four generations in the workplace have on how you will approach work/life balance issues in your workplace?
14. Describe the potential impact that can arise if the integration of the four generations in the workplace is not properly managed.

Section 3 – Cooperative Relationships – Volunteers Wanted

1. The term "volunteer program administrator" is used within this book to describe any person that leads volunteers. Describe why this position is critical to the overall success of an organization's volunteer programs.
2. Describe the ideal volunteer program administrator. Why are the qualities, traits, or characteristics that you listed in your description important?
3. How may the "only a volunteer" mindset influence the behaviors of volunteers? Of paid staff?
4. What are some of the activities performed and benefits derived from volunteers in the various organizations in which they serve?
5. Discuss why it is important to include the vision statement of the organization and the goals of the work unit in the volunteer's "position description."

6. Training in the areas of decision-making, effective oral and written communication techniques, team building, conflict resolution and dealing with stress, anger or trauma are all topics that apply to a wide range of volunteer positions. Evaluate this statement. Do you agree, if so why? If not, why not?

7. Several ideas on rewards and recognition of volunteers were covered. Describe how you would express your gratitude to volunteers and also how you would want to be recognized for your volunteer efforts.

8. What are the benefits of purpose-centered leadership to an organization and its staff?

9. Describe some key leadership qualities that inspire excellence.

10. Review the twelve keys to develop critical thinking skills found in Chapter 10. Choose one key that resonates with you the most and describe how it will influence your actions in the future.

11. Trust can be broken when people sense their leader is smoothing over or condoning someone else's willful and intentional inappropriate behavior. Give an example of why you agree or disagree with this statement.

12. Conflict avoidance never resolves the problem. Evaluate this statement.

13. Describe the steps that you can take to keep your volunteers motivated and supportive of your organization's vision, mission and goals.

APPENDIX B
Universal Declaration on Volunteering

Universal Declaration on Volunteering, adopted by the Board of Directors of the International Association for Volunteer Effort (IAVE), January 2001, The Netherlands.

Volunteering is a fundamental building block of civil society. It brings to life the noblest aspirations of humankind - the pursuit of peace, freedom, opportunity, safety, and justice for all people.

In this era of globalization and continuous change, the world is becoming smaller, more interdependent, and more complex. Volunteering - either through individual or group action - is a way in which:

- human values of community, caring, and serving can be sustained and strengthened;
- individuals can exercise their rights and responsibilities as members of communities, while learning and growing throughout their lives, realizing their full human potential;
- and, connections can be made across differences that push us apart so that we can live together in healthy, sustainable communities, working together to provide innovative solutions to our shared challenges and to shape our collective destinies.

At the dawn of the new millennium, volunteering is an essential element of all societies. It turns into practical, effective action the declaration of the United Nations that "We, the Peoples" have the power to change the world.

This Declaration supports the right of every woman, man and child to associate freely and to volunteer regardless of their cultural and ethnic origin, religion, age, gender, and physical, social or economic condition. All people in the world should have the right to freely offer their time, talent, and energy to others and to their communities through individual and collective action, without expectation of financial reward.

We seek the development of volunteering that:

- elicits the involvement of the entire community in identifying and addressing its problems;
- encourages and enables youth to make leadership through service a continuing part of their lives;
- provides a voice for those who cannot speak for themselves;
- enables others to participate as volunteers;
- complements but does not substitute for responsible action by other sectors and the efforts of paid workers;
- enables people to acquire new knowledge and skills and to fully develop their personal potential, self-reliance and creativity;
- promotes family, community, national and global solidarity.

We believe that volunteers and the organizations and communities that they serve have a shared responsibility to:

- create environments in which volunteers have meaningful work that helps to achieve agreed upon results;
- define the criteria for volunteer participation, including the conditions under which the organization and the volunteer may end their commitment, and develop policies to guide volunteer activity;
- provide appropriate protections against risks for volunteers and those they serve:
- provide volunteers with appropriate training, regular evaluation, and recognition;
- ensure access for all by removing physical, economic, social, and cultural barriers to their participation.

Taking into account basic human rights as expressed in the United Nations Declaration on Human Rights, the principles of volunteering and the responsibilities of volunteers and the organizations in which they are involved, we call on:

All volunteers to proclaim their belief in volunteer action as a creative and mediating force that:

- builds healthy, sustainable communities that respect the dignity of all people;
- empowers people to exercise their rights as human beings and, thus, to improve their lives;
- helps solve social, cultural, economic and environmental problems; and,
- builds a more humane and just society through worldwide cooperation.

The leaders of:

- all sectors to join together to create strong, visible, and effective local and national "volunteer centres" as the primary leadership organizations for volunteering;
- government to ensure the rights of all people to volunteer, to remove any legal barriers to participation, to engage volunteers in its work, and to provide resources to NGOs to promote and support the effective mobilization and management of volunteers;
- business to encourage and facilitate the involvement of its workers in the community as volunteers and to commit human and financial resources to develop the infrastructure needed to support volunteering;
- the media to tell the stories of volunteers and to provide information that encourages and assists people to volunteer;
- education to encourage and assist people of all ages to volunteer, creating opportunities for them to reflect on and learn from their service;
- religion to affirm volunteering as an appropriate response to the spiritual call to all people to serve;
- NGOs to create organizational environments that are friendly to volunteers and to commit the human and

financial resources that are required to effectively engage volunteers.

The United Nations to:
- declare this to be the "Decade of Volunteers and Civil Society" in recognition of the need to strengthen the institutions of free societies; and,
- recognize the "red V" as the universal symbol for volunteering.

IAVE challenges volunteers and leaders of all sectors throughout the world to unite as partners to promote and support effective volunteering, accessible to all, as a symbol of solidarity among all peoples and nations. IAVE invites the global volunteer community to study, discuss, endorse and bring into being this Universal Declaration on Volunteering.

Adopted by the international board of directors of IAVE - The International Association for Volunteer Effort at its 16th World Volunteer Conference, Amsterdam, The Netherlands, January 2001, the International Year of Volunteers.

BIBLIOGRAPHY

Adams, Karen Blanks. *Life in the Matrix: Are you really in control of your decisions?* Lake Mary, FL: Creation House, 2010.

Augsburger, David. *Caring Enough to Confront.* Ventura: Regal Books, 1981.

Bill Bennett, COO The McNeill Group. "Is "JOE" Making the Decisions Which Will Produce the Best Results?" *The Quantum Leader: Your Success is Our Business,* 2011.

Borisoff, Deborah, and David A Victor. *Conflict Management: A Communication Skill Approach, Second Edition.* Needham Heights, MA: Allyn & Bacon, 1989.

Buckingham, Marcus, Clifton, Donald O, Ph.D. *Now Discover Your Strengths.* New York: The Free Press, 2001.

Buller, David, and Judee Burgoon. "Interpersonal Deception Theory." In *A First Look at Communication Theory, Sixth Edition,* by Em Griffin, 97-109. New York: The McGraw-Hill Companies, Inc., 2006.

Bunker, Barbara Benedict. "Managing Conflict Through Large-Group Methods." In *The Handbook of Conflict Resolution: Theory and Practice, Second Edition,* by Morton Deutsch, Peter T Coleman and Eric Marcus, 764. San Francisco: Jossey-Bass, 2006.

CLC, Corporate Leadership Council. *Driving Performance and Retention Throught Employee Engagement.* Strategic Research, Washington, DC: Corporate Leadership Council, 2004.

Das, Subhamoy. *5 Principles & 10 Disciplines: The Basics of Hinduism.* 1999. http://hinduism.about.com/od/basics/a/principles.htm (accessed November 25, 2011).

DeKoven, Stan E, Ph.D. *Christian Education Principles & Practice.* Ramona, CA: Vision Publishing, 1996.

Donohue, William A, Kolt, Robert. *Managing Interpersonal Conflict.* Newbury Park, CA: Sage Publications, Inc., 1992.

Emery, Merrelyn, and R. E. Purser. *The Search Conference: A Powerful Method for Planning Organizational Change and Community Action.* San Francisco: Jossey-Bass, 1996.

Fisher, James C, and Kathleen M Cole. *Leadership and Management of Volunteer Programs: A Guide for Volunteer Administrators.* San Francisco: Jossey-Bass, Inc., 1993.

Fundamental Buddhism. 1997. http://www.fundamental buddhism.com/noble-eighthold-path.html (accessed November 25, 2011).

Gangel, Kenneth O, and Samuel A Canine. *Communication and Conflict Management in Churches and Christian Organizations.* Eugene: Wipf and Stock Publishers, 1992.

Getzels, J. W., and E. G. Guba. "Social Behavior and the Administrative Process." In *Communication and Conflict Management in Churches and Christian Organizations*, by Kenneth O Gangel and Samuel A Canine, 27-28. Eugene: Wipf and Stock Publishers, 2002.

Griffin, Em. *A First Look at Communication Theory, Second Edition.* New York: The McGraw-Hill Companies, Inc., 1994.

Griffin, Em. "Attribution Theory of Fritz Heider." In *A First Look at Communication Theory, Second Edition*, by Em Griffin, 137-146. New York: McGraw-Hill Companies, Inc., 1994.

Griffin, Emory M. *Making Friends & Making Them Count.* Downers Grove, IL: InterVarsity Press, 1987.

Gudykunst, William B. "An Anxiety/Uncertainty Management (AUM) Theory of Effective CommunicationLMaking the Mesh of the Net Finder." In *Theorizing About Intercultural Communication*, by William B Gudykunst, 289. Thousand Oaks, CA: Sage, 2005.

Hammond, Sue Annis. *The Thin Book of Appreciative Inquiry, Second Edition.* Plano, TX: Thin Book Publishing Company, 1996.

Hill, Charles W L. *International Business: Competing in the Global Marketplace, Fifth Edition.* New York: The McGraw-Hill Companies, Inc., 2005.

Hofstede, Geert. "Culture's Consequences: International Differences in Work Related Values." In *International Business: Competing in the Global Marketplace, Fifth Edition*, by Charles W L Hill, 88-121. New York: The McGraw-Hill Companies, Inc., 2005.

Hunger, J. David, and Thomas L Wheelen. *Essentials of Strategic Management, Third Edition.* Upper Saddle River, NJ: Pearson Education, Inc., 2003.

IAVE, International Association of Volunteer Efforts. *The Universal Declaration on Volunteering.* September 25, 2009. http://www.iave.org/content/universal-declaration-volunteering (accessed December 7, 2011).

Inscape. *DiSC Classic - Corexcel Company.* 1996. http://www.corexcel.com/ disc_profile_ebrochure.pdf (accessed December 6, 2011).

Interaction Associates, LLC. "Introduction to The Interaction Method." *Essential Facilitation Core Skills for Guiding Groups.* Dallas: Interaction Associates, LLC, 2003. Sections 2:1-20; 6:1-44.

Janis, I. *Groupthink: Psychological Studies of Policy Decisions and Fiascos.* Boston: Houghton-Miflin, 1982.

Janis, Irving. "Groupthink." In *A First Look at Communication Theory, 3rd Edition*, by Em Griffin, 235-246. New York: The McGraw-Hill Companies, Inc., 1997.

Keirsey, David. *Please Understand Me II: Temperament, Character, Intelligence.* Del Mar, CA: Prometheus Nemesis Book Company, 1998.

Krauss, Robert M, and Ezequiel Morsella. "Communication and Conflict." In *The Handbook of Conflict Resolution: Theory and Practice, Second Edition*, by Morton Deutsch, Peter T Coleman and Eric C Marcus, 150-152. San Francisco: Jossey-Bass, 2006.

Lee, Jarene Frances, and Julia M Catagnus. *Supervising Volunteers: An Action Guide for Making Your Job Easier.* Philadelphia: Energize, Inc., 1999.

Li, Charlene, and Josh Bernoff. *groundswell: winning in a world transformed by social technologies.* Boston: Harvard Business School Publishing, 2008.

MacLeod, Flora, and Sarah Hogarth. *Leading Today's Volunteers: Motivate and Manage Your Team, Second Edition.* Birminham, WA: International Self-Counsel Press Ltd., 1999.

Maldonado, Guillermo. *Leaders tha Conquer*. GM Ministries, 2004.

—. *Leaders that Conquer*. GM Ministries, 2004.

McKee, Jonathan, McKee, Thomas W. *The New Breed: Understanding & Equipping the 21st Century Volunteer*. Loveland, CO: Group, 2008.

Myers, Isabel. "The Myers-Brigg Indicator." In *Please Understand Me II*, by David Keirsey, 2-16. Del Mar, CA: Prometheus Nemesis Book Company, 1998.

Peterson, Eugene. *THE MESSAGE: The Bible in Contemporary Language*. Colorado Springs: NavPress Publishing Group, 2002.

Pierce, Chuck D. *God's Unfolding Battle Plan: A Field Manual for Advancing the Kingdom of God*. Ventura, CA: Regal Books, 2007.

Sande, Ken. *The Peacemaker: A Biblical Guide to Resolving Personal Conflict*. Grand Rapids: Baker Books, 2004.

Schramm, Wilbur. *The Process and Effects of Communication*. Urbana: University of Illinois Press, 1954.

—. *The Process and Effects of Mass Communication*. Urbana: The University of Illinois Press, 1961.

Schultz, William. "FIRO Theory of Needs." In *A First Look at Communication Theory, First Edition*, by Em Griffin, 93-101. New York: The McGraw-Hill Companies, Inc., 1991.

Sepulveda, Art. *Focus: what's in your vision?* Tulsa, OK: Harrison House, Inc., 2004.

Shannon, Claude, and Warren Weaver. "The Mathematical Theory of Communication." In *A First Look at Communication Theory, Seventh Edition*, by Em Griffin, 44. New York: McGraw-Hill Companies, Inc., 2009.

Shawchuck, Norman. *How to Manage Conflict in the Church*. Irvine, CA: Spiritual Growth Resources, 1983.

Sire, James W. *The Universe Next Door, Fifth Edition*. Downers Grove, IL: InterVarsity Press, 2009.

The American Heritage College Dictionary, Fourth Edition. Boston: Houghton Mifflin Company, 2007.

The Holy Bible, New International Version. Grand Rapids: Zondervan, 1984.

Thompson, Leigh, Janice Nadler, and Robert B Jr. Lount. "Judgmental Biases in Conflict Resolution and How to Overcome Them." In *The Handbook of Conflict Resolution: Theory and Practice*, by Morton Deutsch, Peter T Coleman and Eric C Marcus, 249-250. San Francisco: Jossey-Bass, 2006.

Tylor, Edward B. "Primitive Culture." In *International Business: Competing in the Global Marketplace, Fifth Edition*, by Charles W L Hill, 88-124. New York: The McGraw-Hill Companies, Inc, 2005.

Ury, William. *Getting Past No: Negotiating Your Way From Confrontation to Cooperation.* New York: Bantam Book, 1991.

Van Yperen, Jim. *Making Peace: A Guide to Overcoming Church Conflict.* Chicago: Moody Publishers, 2002.

Wagner, C. Peter, Ph.D. *The New Apostolic Reformation.* August 18, 2011. www.globalspheres.org (accessed November 16, 2011).

INDEX OF KEY TERMS

CPSIA information can be obtained at www.ICGtesting.com
Printed in the USA
LVOW100546030712

288615LV00002B/3/P